Havana, Cuba

Havana, Cuba - March 2012
Photographs and captions by Tomi Murphy
Edited by Rachel Murphy

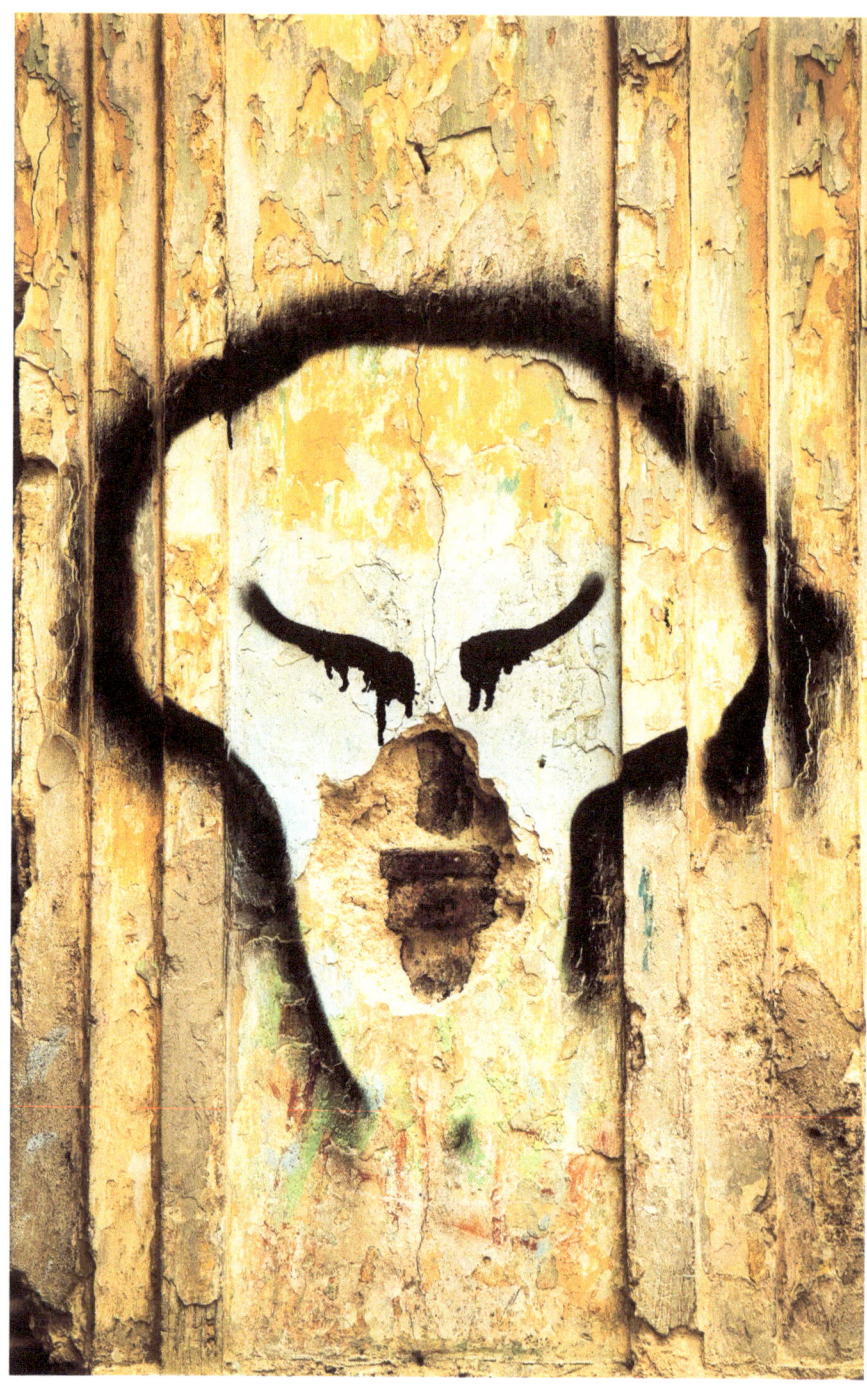

There are many old buildings in Old Havana. While some of them are being restored, many of them coninue to deteriorate and some do not even seem safe to occupy. Yet, people continue to live there.

And despite these conditions in which they live, the people of Havana are surprisingly civil, polite, and hospitable. Even more surprisingly, they are so friendly, cheerful, and seem to have a good sense of humor.

Take this picture, for example, a hole in the wall of a crumbling building is turned into a work of art!

Go ahead.
Turn the page.

Get to know Old Havana and the amazing people who live there.

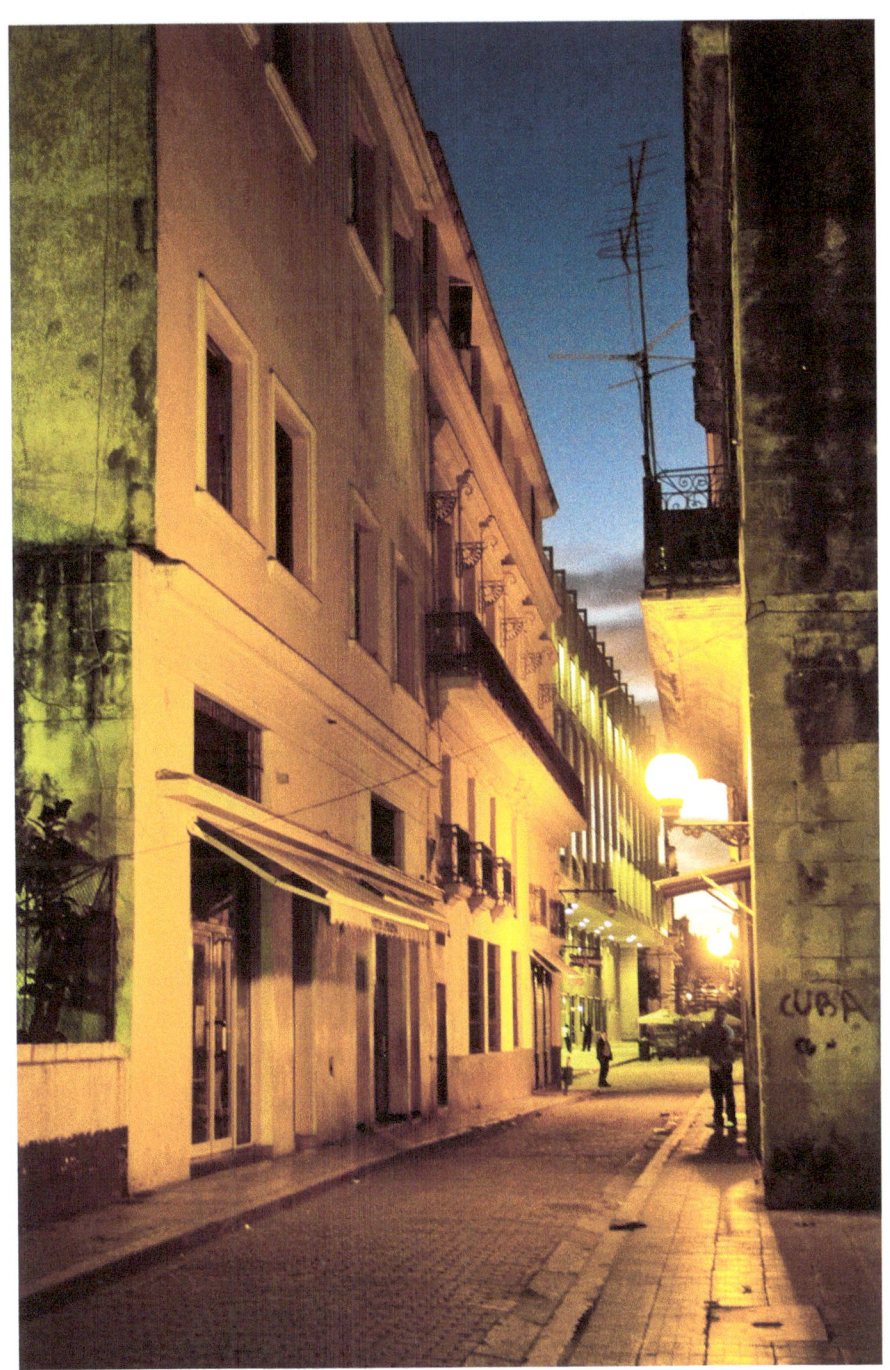

The day starts at 6 am. People are outside washing the street in front of their shops, getting ready for another day.

Garbage trucks are buzzing around, chasing off the dogs enjoying some restaurant scraps.

Soon, the sun will be up and these streets will be bustling with people headed to work.

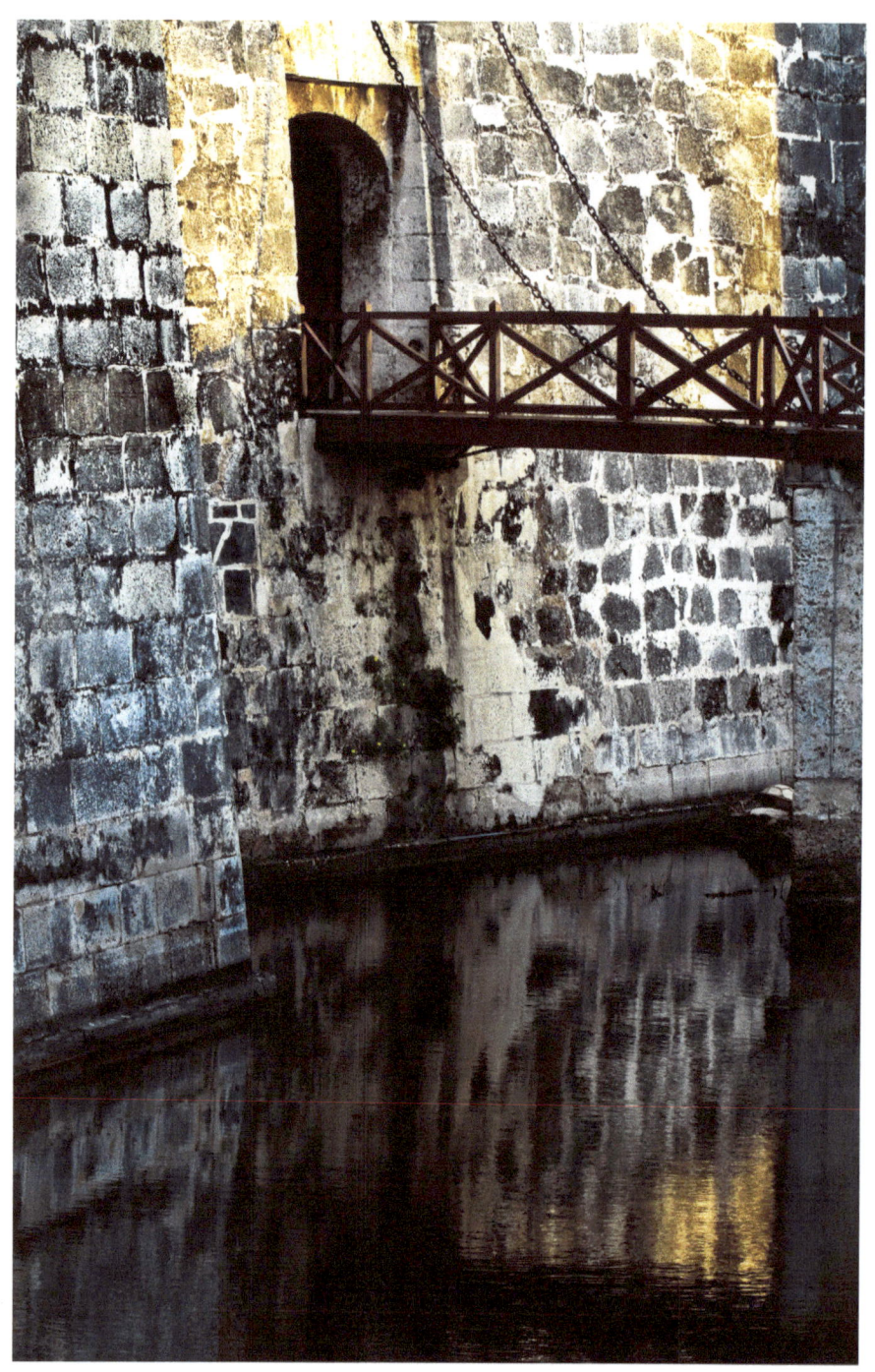

Early morning sun is
warming up the old
castle wall.

*Castillo de La Real
Fuerza
(Castle of Royal Force)*

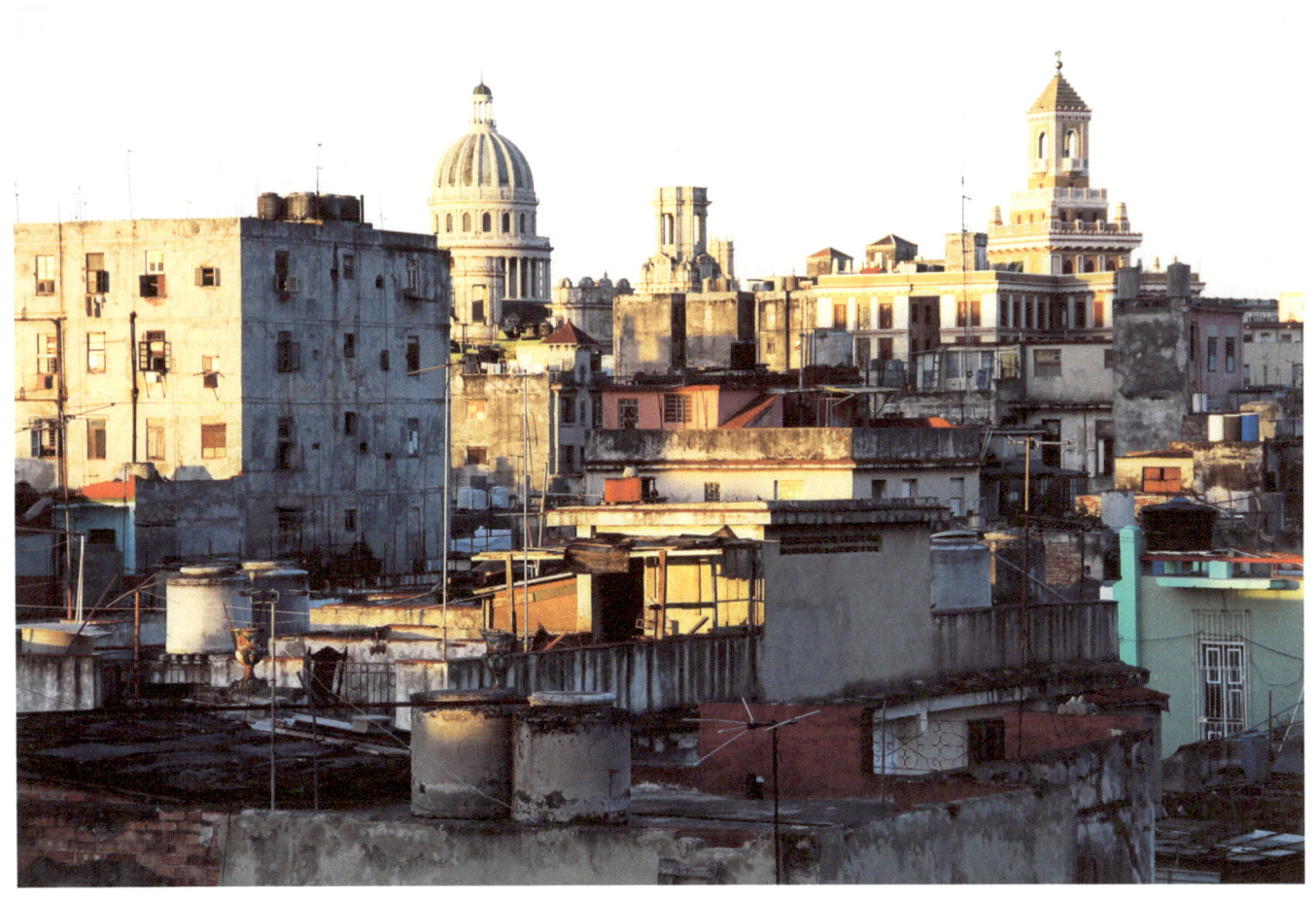

Here, the warm sun wakes up the whole city and reveals colors hidden in the night.

It also reveals the stark contrast between well-maintained structures like the Capital and Bacardi buildings and the crumbling apartments that house the residents.

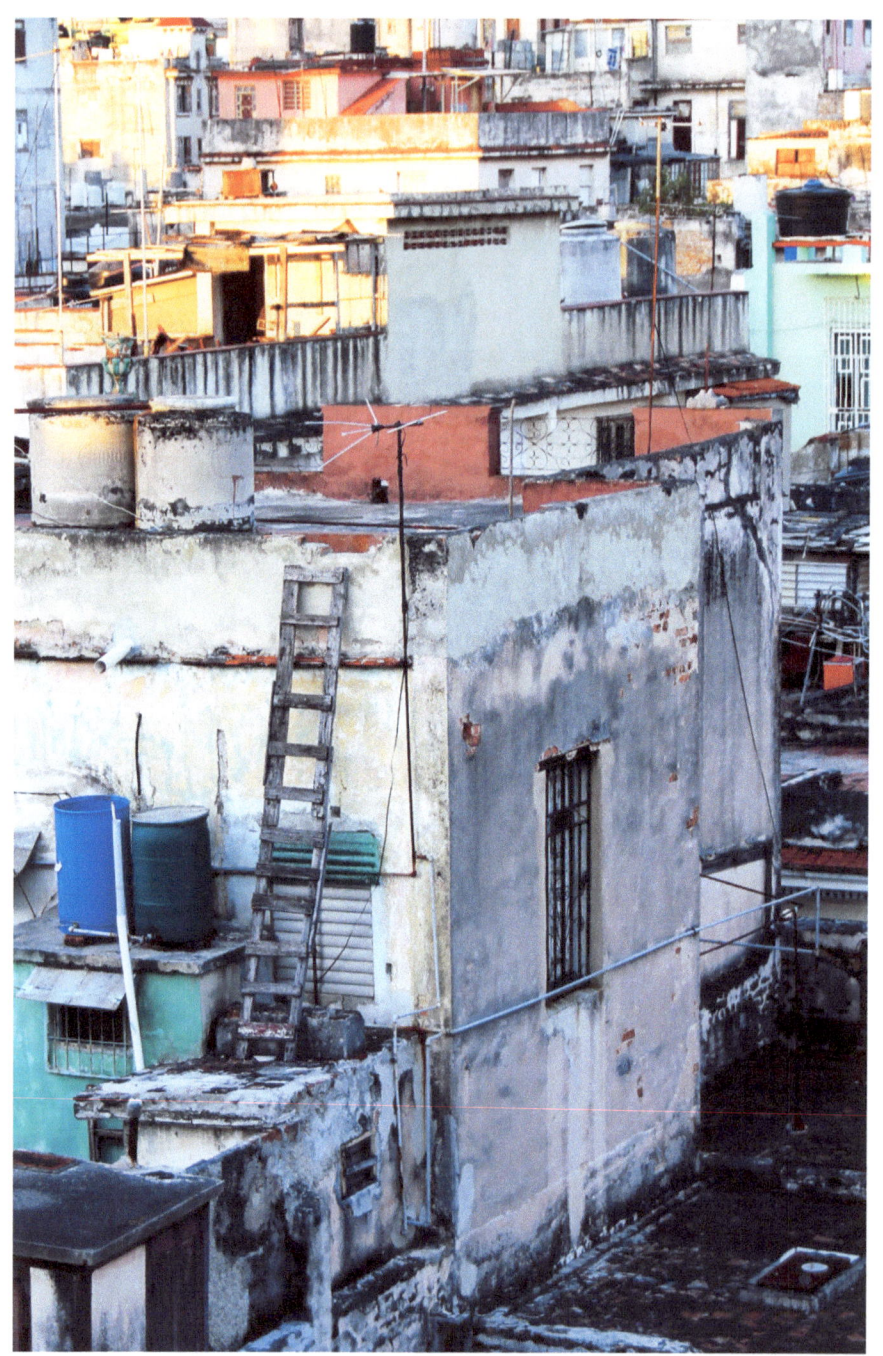

Come closer. Take a look at the condition of these buildings.

I hope they don't have to go up that ladder to fix the TV antenna very often...

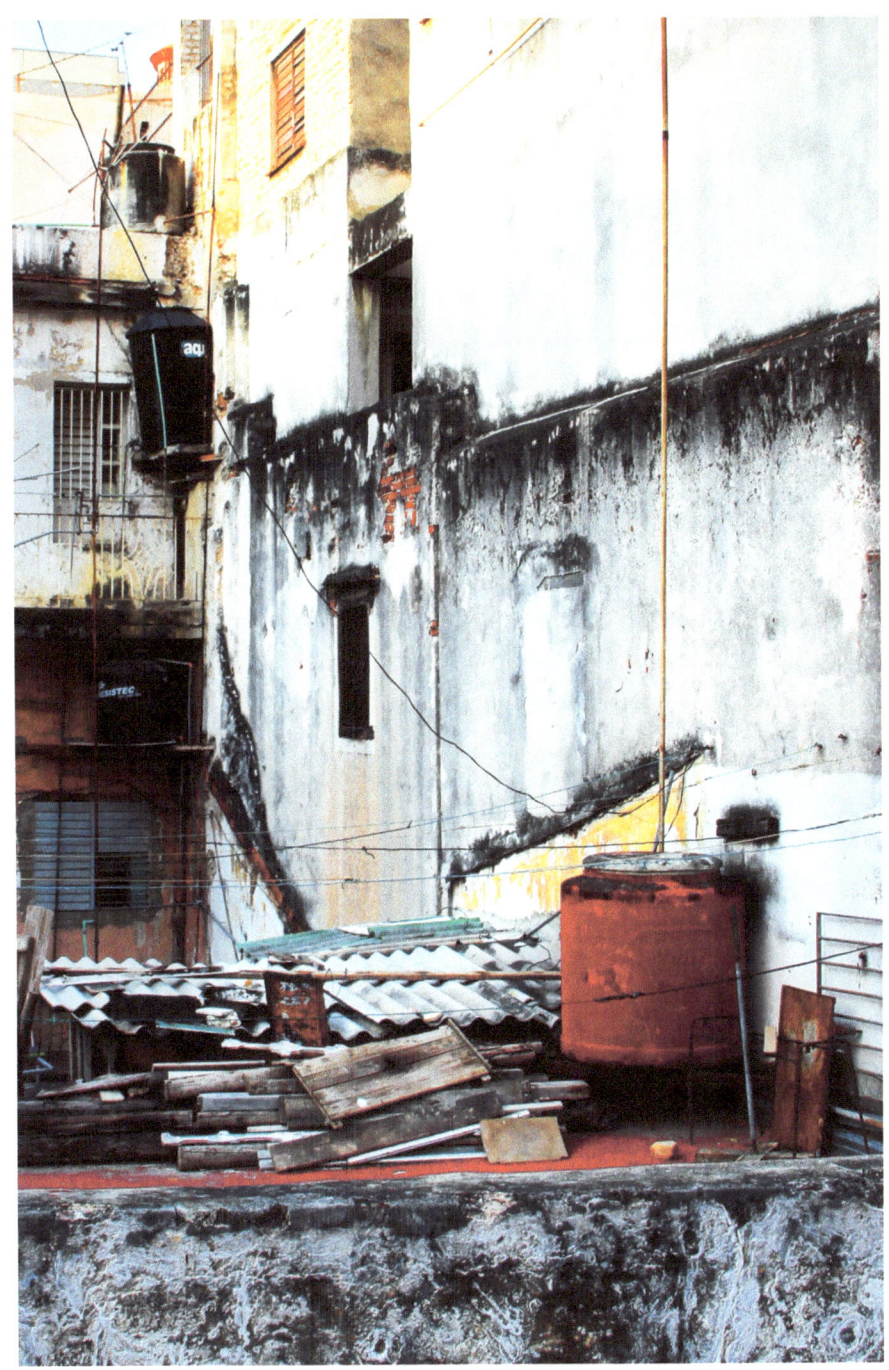

There is art and color everywhere in Havana.

Among a pile of old build-ing materials, a red water drum sits like a queen demanding attention. But even this queen cannot completely dis-tract from the ailing con-dition of these buildings.

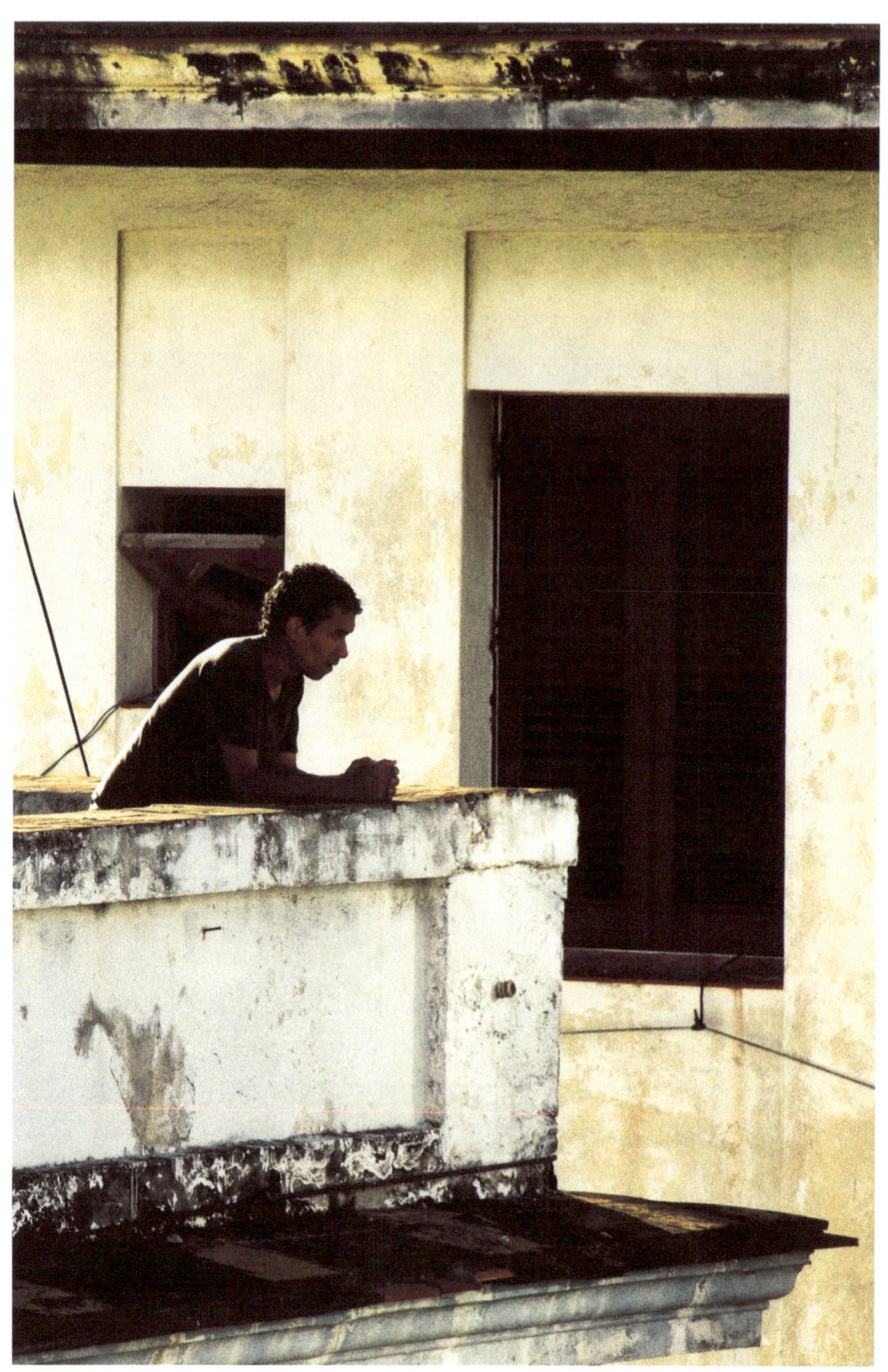

Living in Cuba is tough, especially for young people. While the government provides excellent education and healthcare, access to the outside world is very limited.

Many of them can only dream.

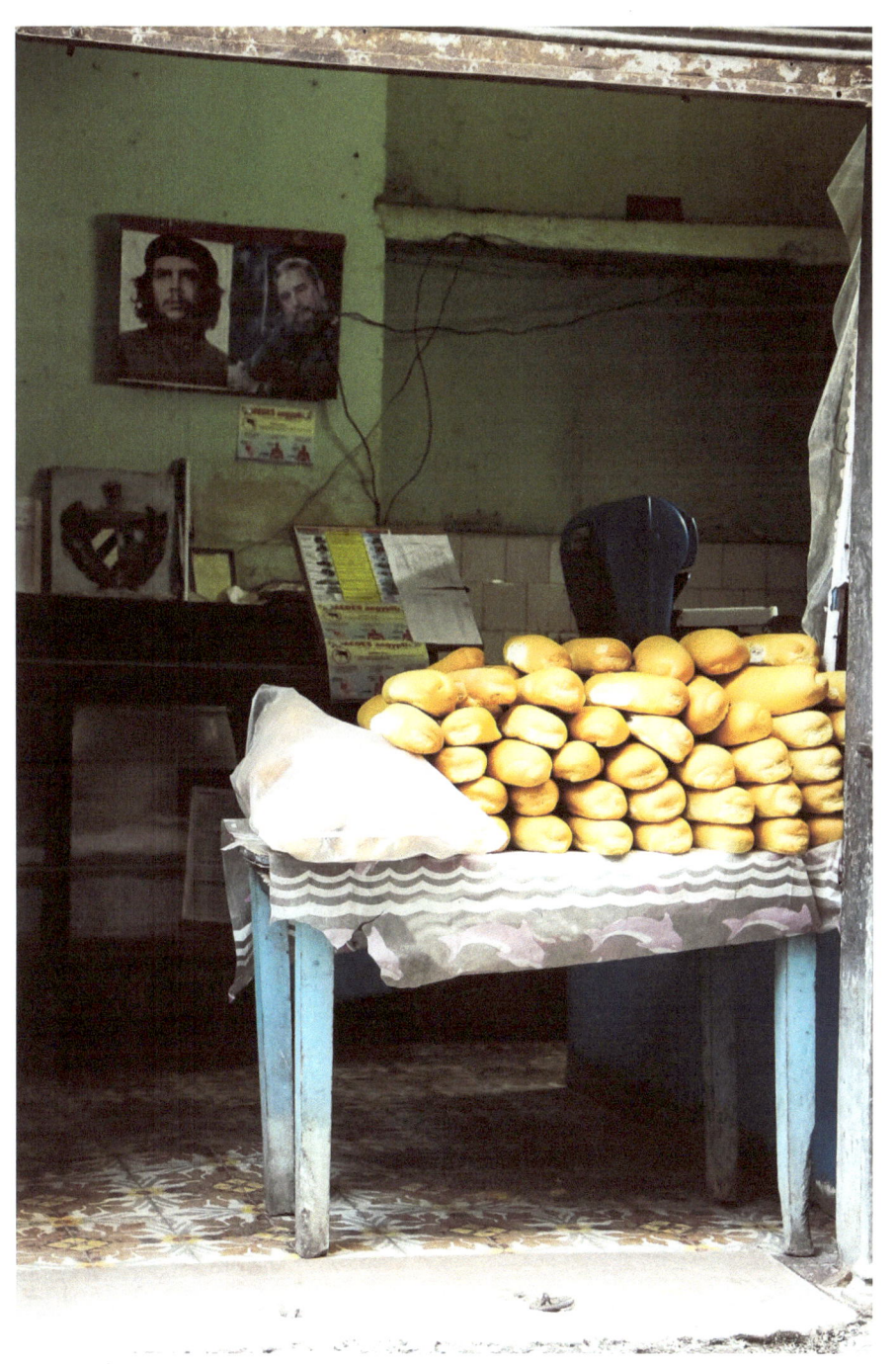

Early in the morning, shops like this fill the streets with the wonderful smell of freshly baked bread.

On the wall behind the bread hang pictures of Che Guevara and Fidel Castro. Not only are these images sold on all sorts of souvenir items for visitors, they are also displayed by many businesses to show their affection and respect for the revolutionaries.

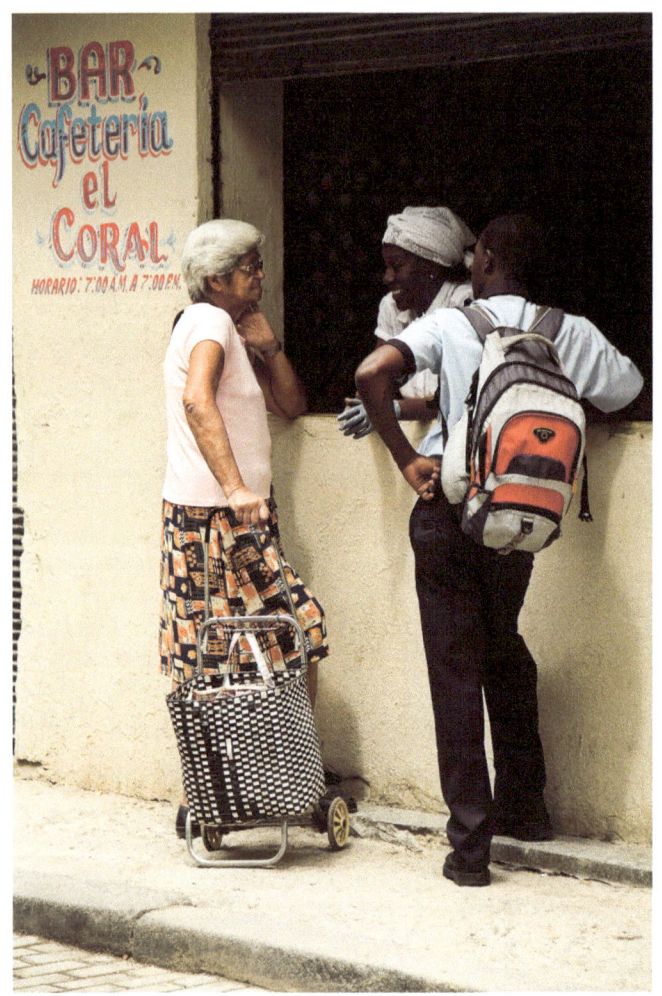 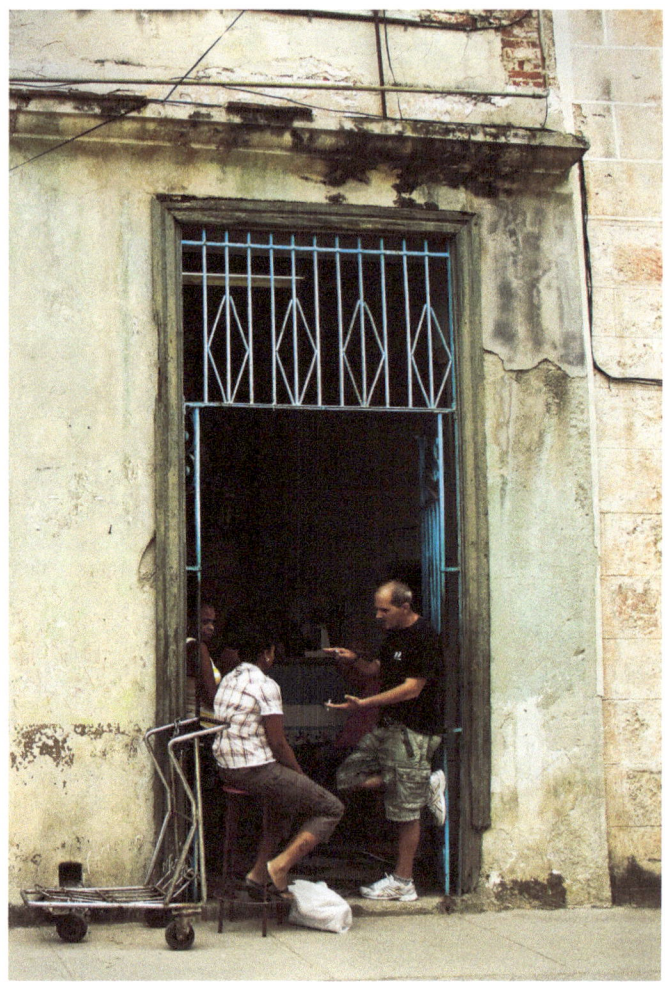

Little cafes selling sweet buns, coffee, or anything else, perfectly showcase the friendly and communal character of Cuban people. They are often engaged in some sort of discussion, but whether friendly or serious, there are always smiles.

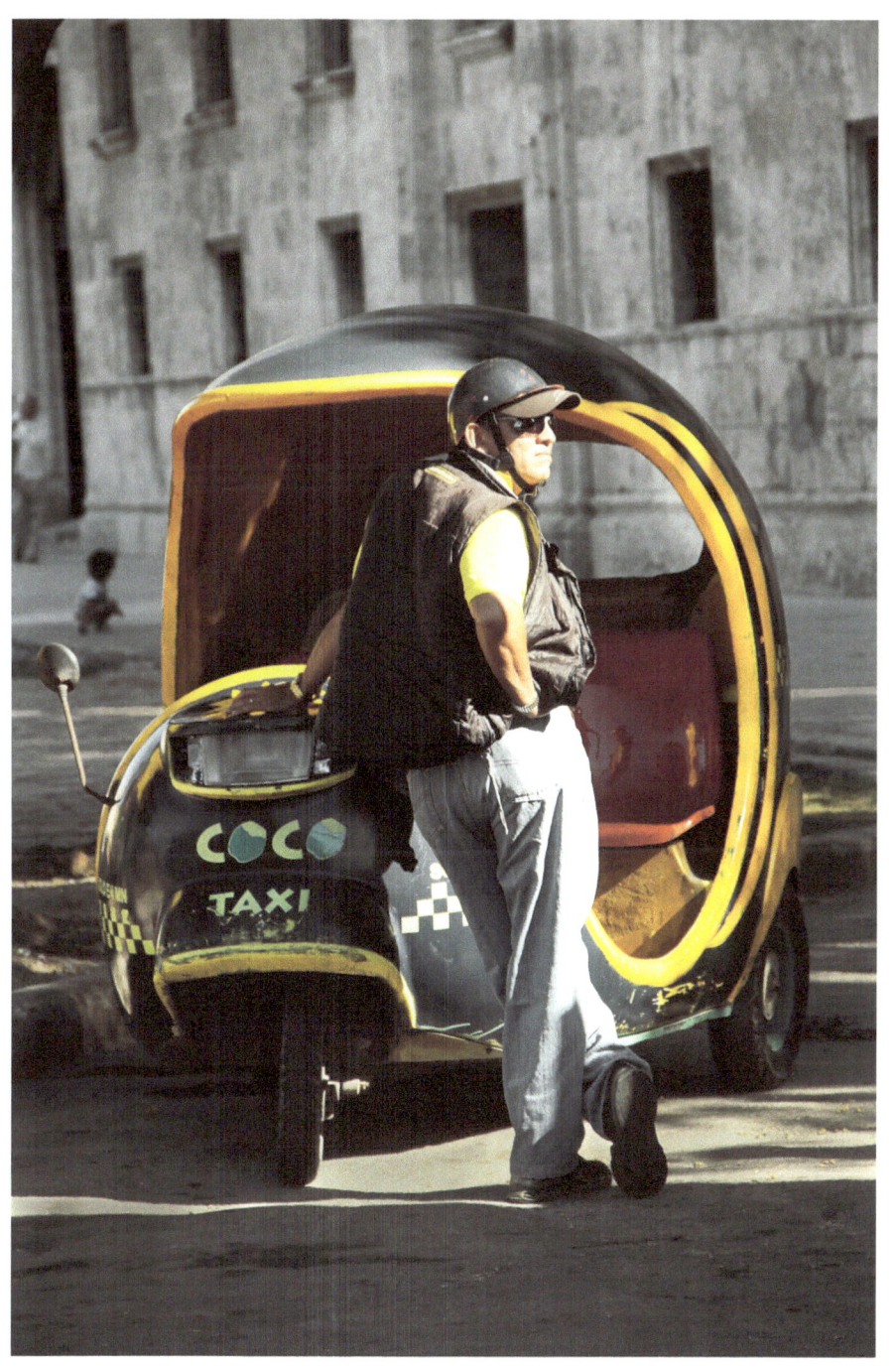

You may know that Cuba is full of beautifully restored classic American cars. You may know that some of those even operate as taxi cabs.

But did you know that in addition to those cabs, there is also this little "CoCo Taxi"? These little cars do not go very fast, do not shield you from the rain, and could potentially tip over if the driver makes a turn too quickly. However, they are so cute and convenient, those other issues don't matter.

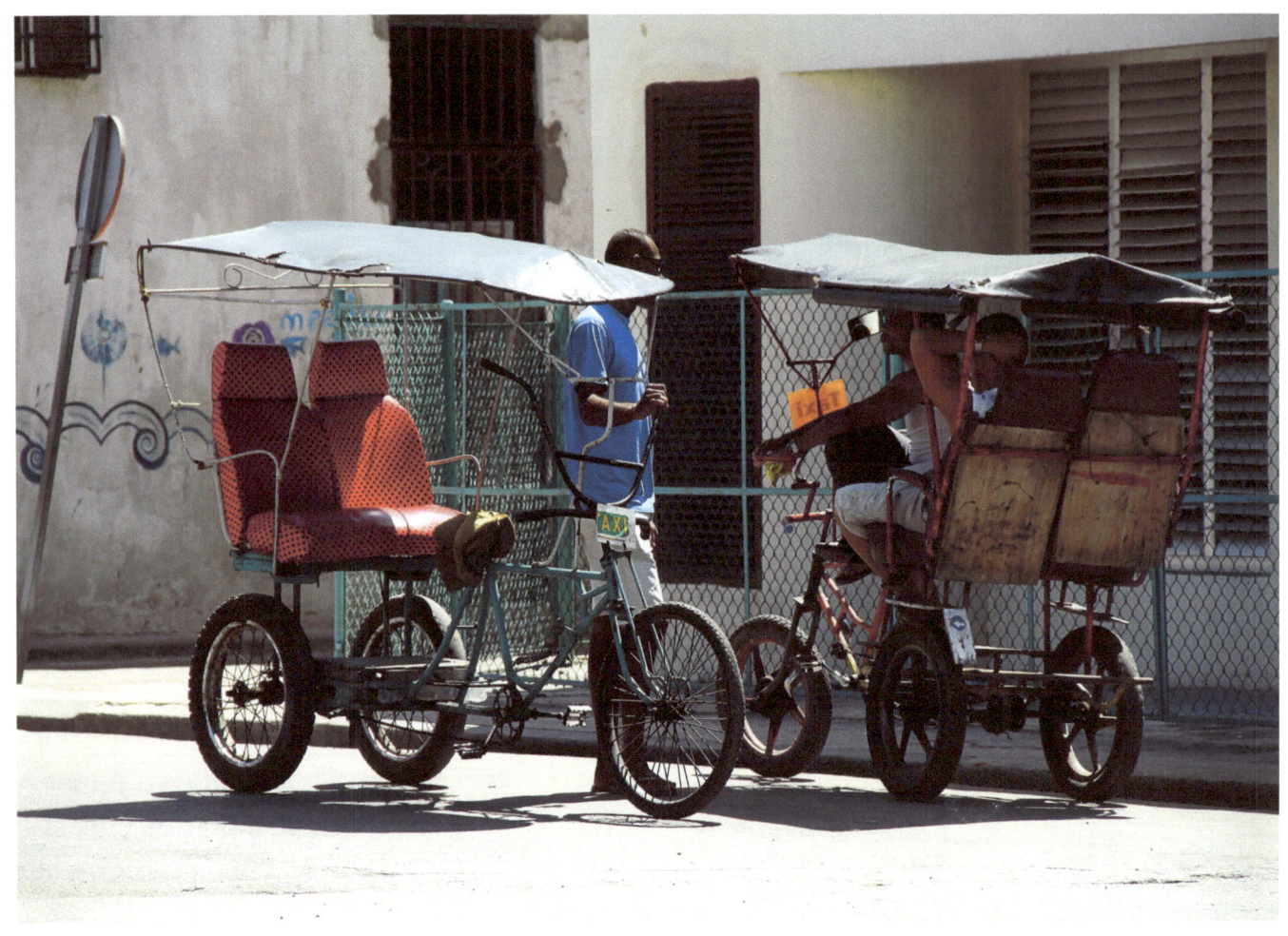

Another method of transportation is the bike taxi. Comfort may be uncertain, but it takes you where you need to go (so long as it's not too far).

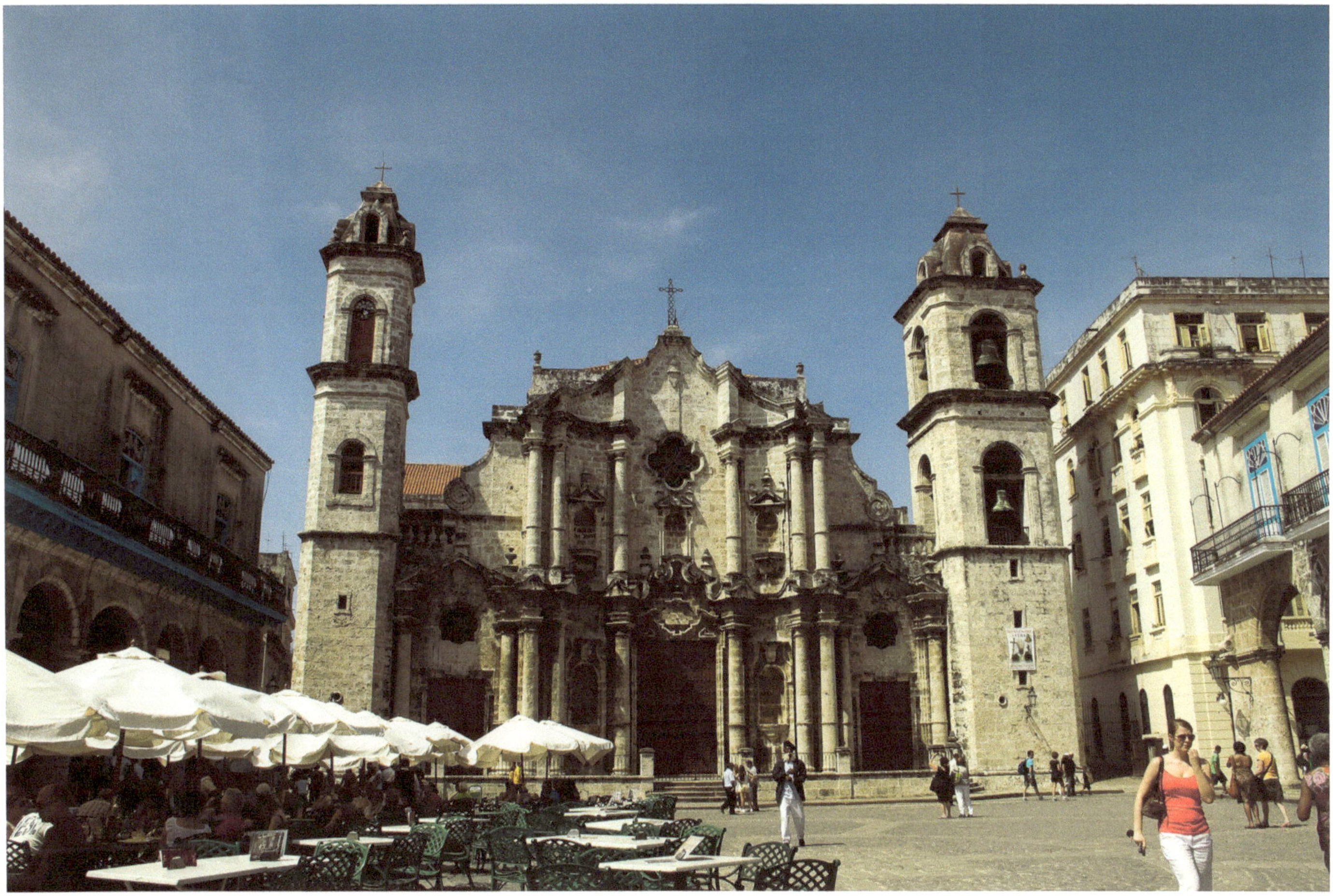

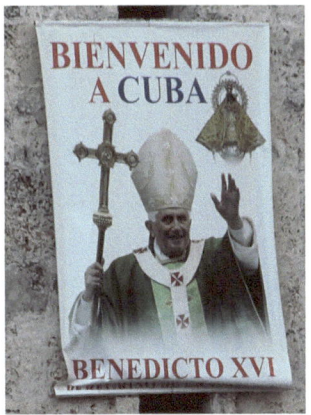

Most of the buildings in Viejo Plaza are in good shape, such as San Cristobal Cathedral.

Before 1959, more than 80% of Cubans were known to be Catholic. The poster on the bell tower advertises the Pope's upcoming visit. Raul Castro has honored an appeal by Pope Benedict XVI and declared this year's Good Friday a public holiday for the first time since Fidel Castro banned religious holidays 53 years ago. Whether this will become an annual holiday is yet to be determined.

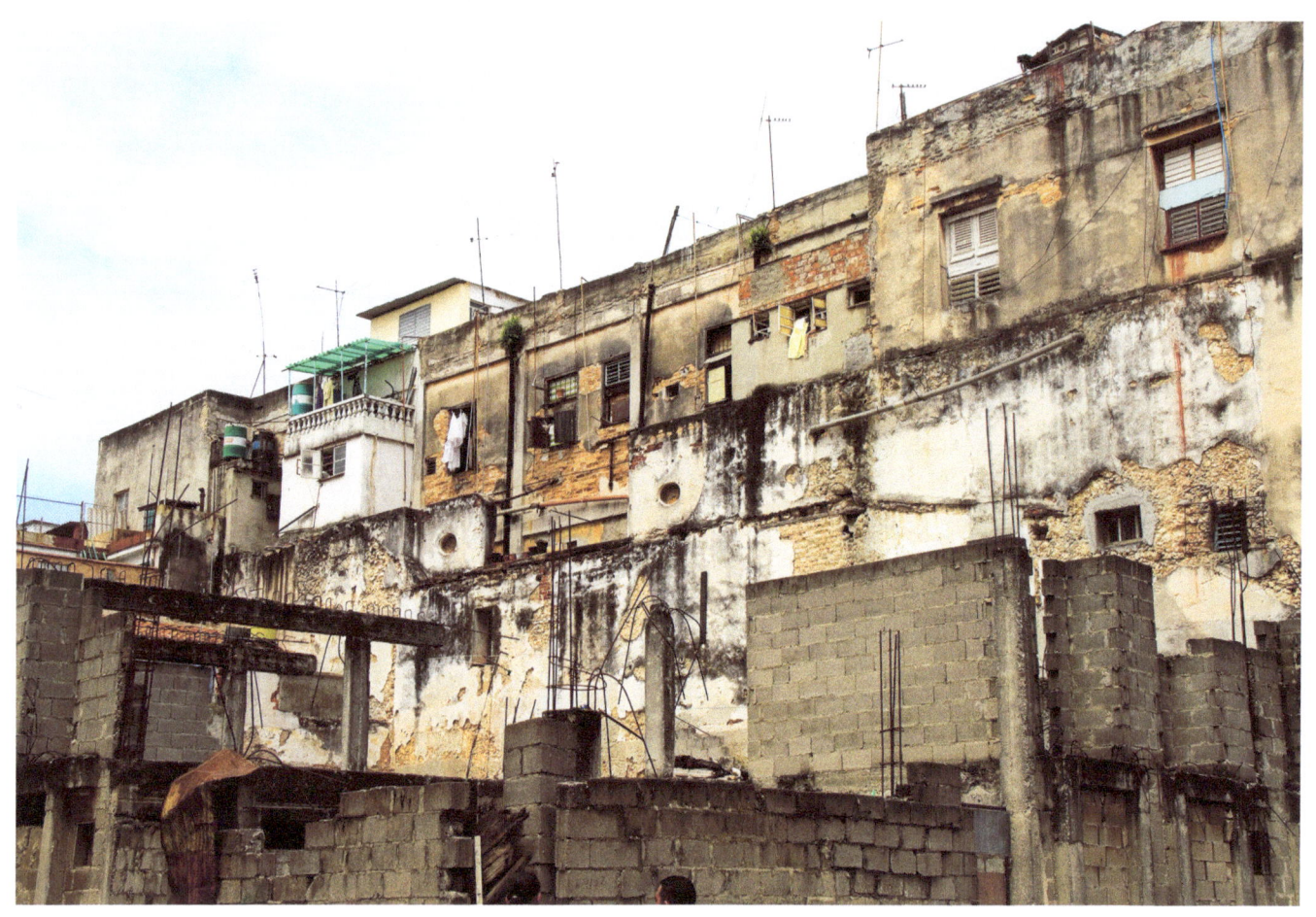

Here is a building (or maybe a cluster of buildings) that looks as if some restoration work was perhaps started, but never finished.

Yet, within this cluster, you still find a green awning next to matching green and white water drums, once again exemplifying how the mundane can be transformed into art.

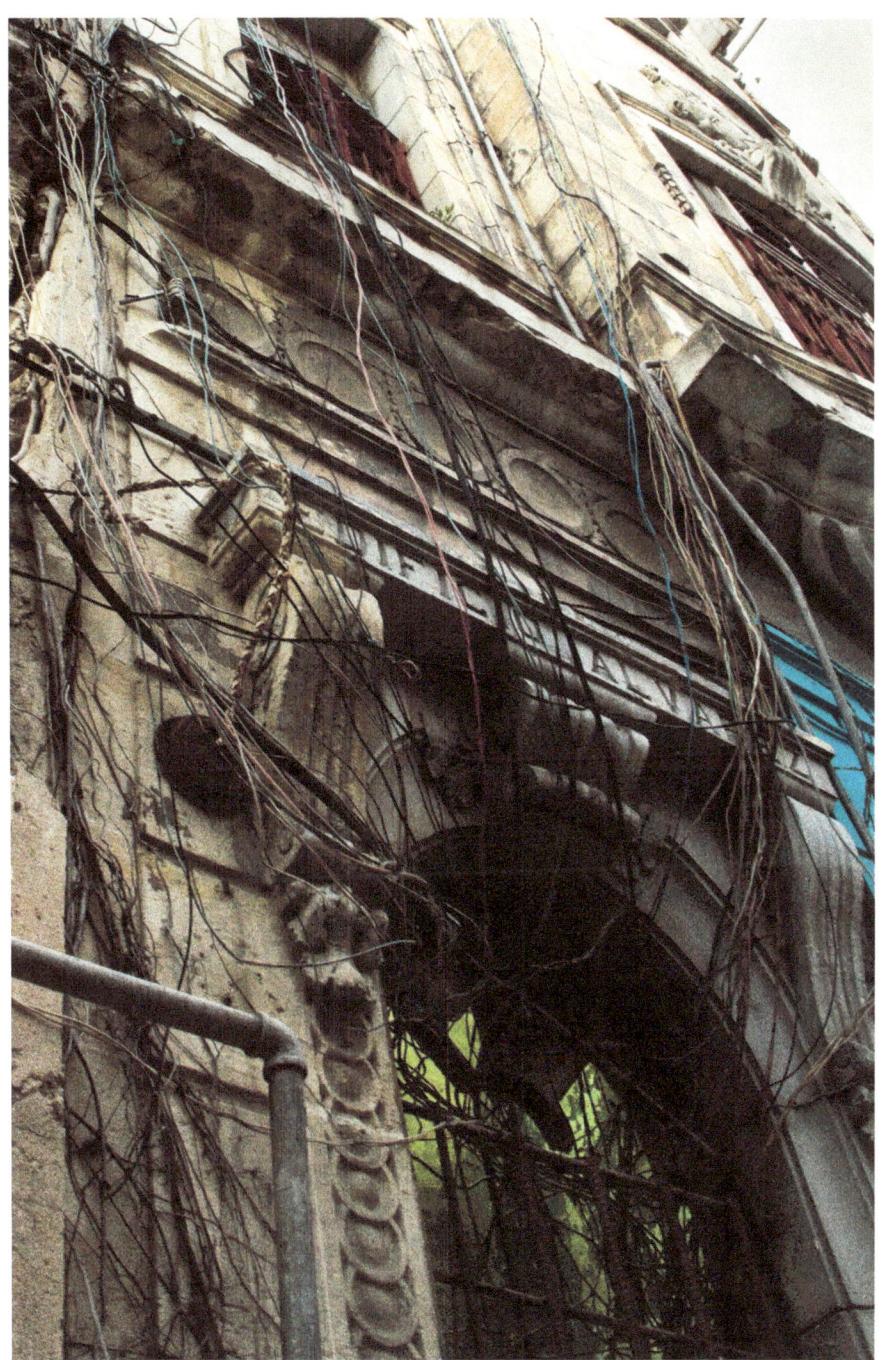

From far away these buildings look like they've been painted with colorful stripes, but as you get closer you realize those stripes are actually electrical wires, sustaining the homes of dozens of families.

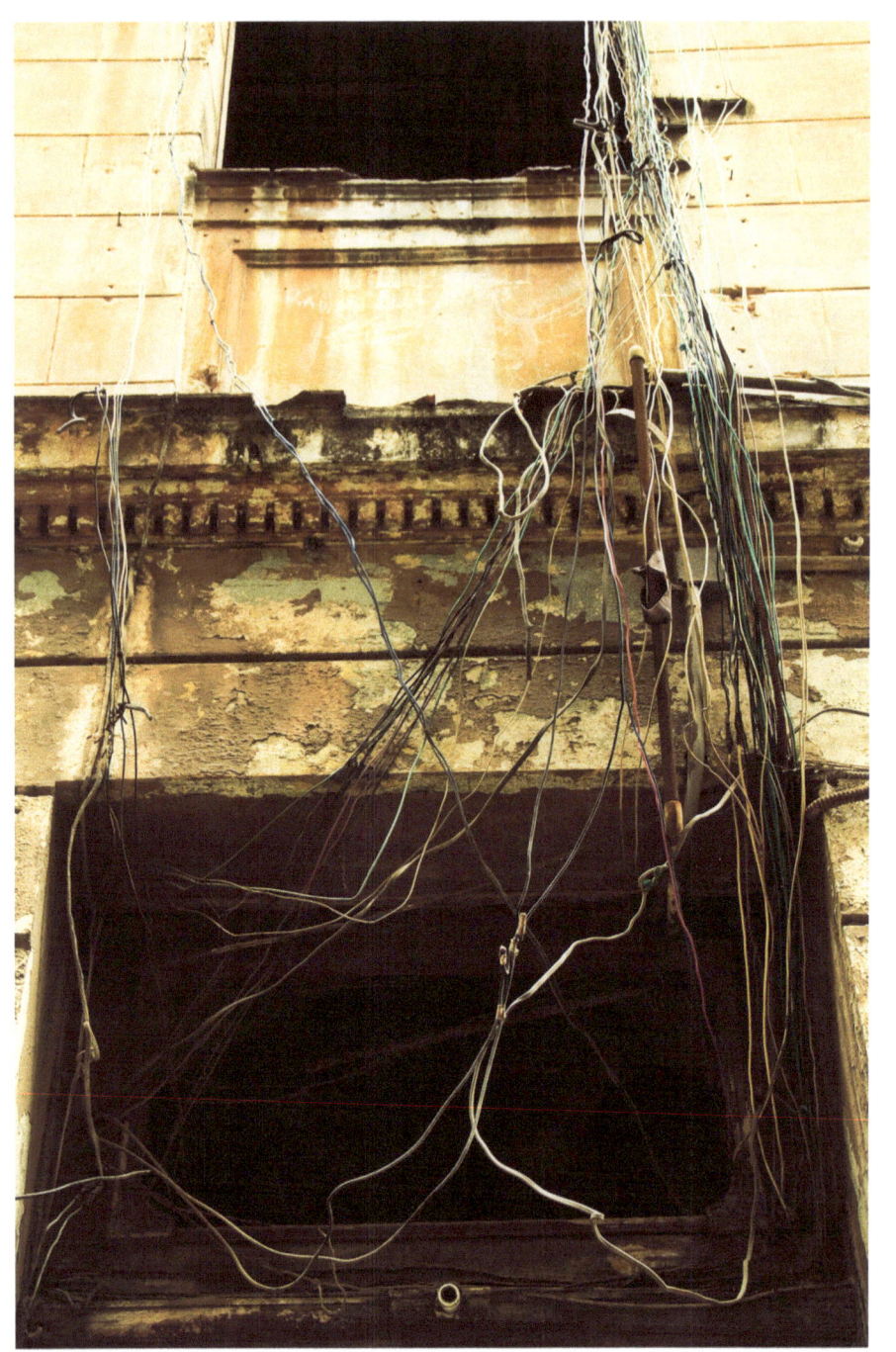

It's almost unbelievable that people live in such dangerous conditions, but they do what they must to survive.

The question is: How much longer do they have to live this way?

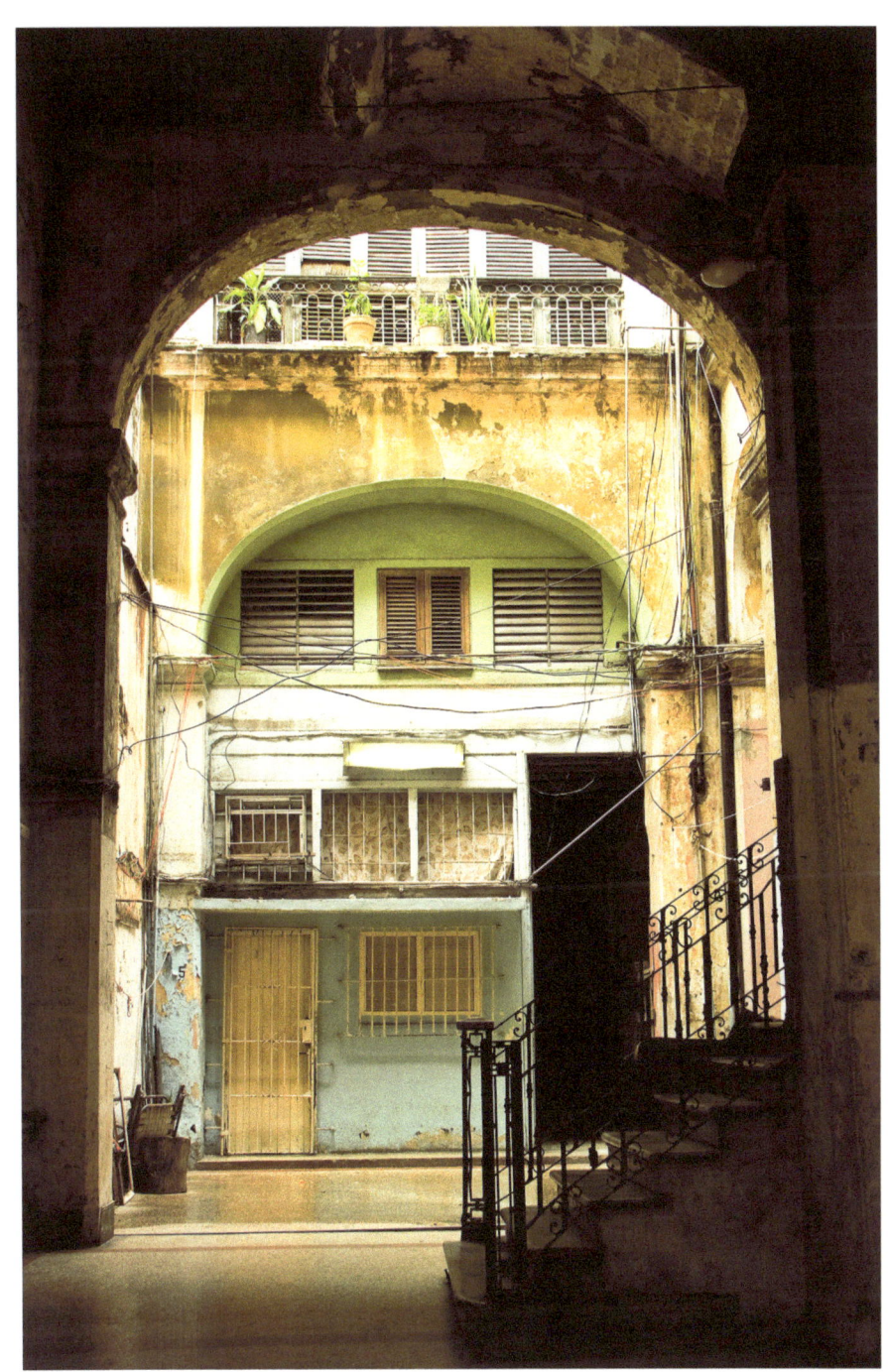

Most apartment buildings have large double doors that are closed at night.

In the daytime, they open up to reveal sunny courtyards like this.

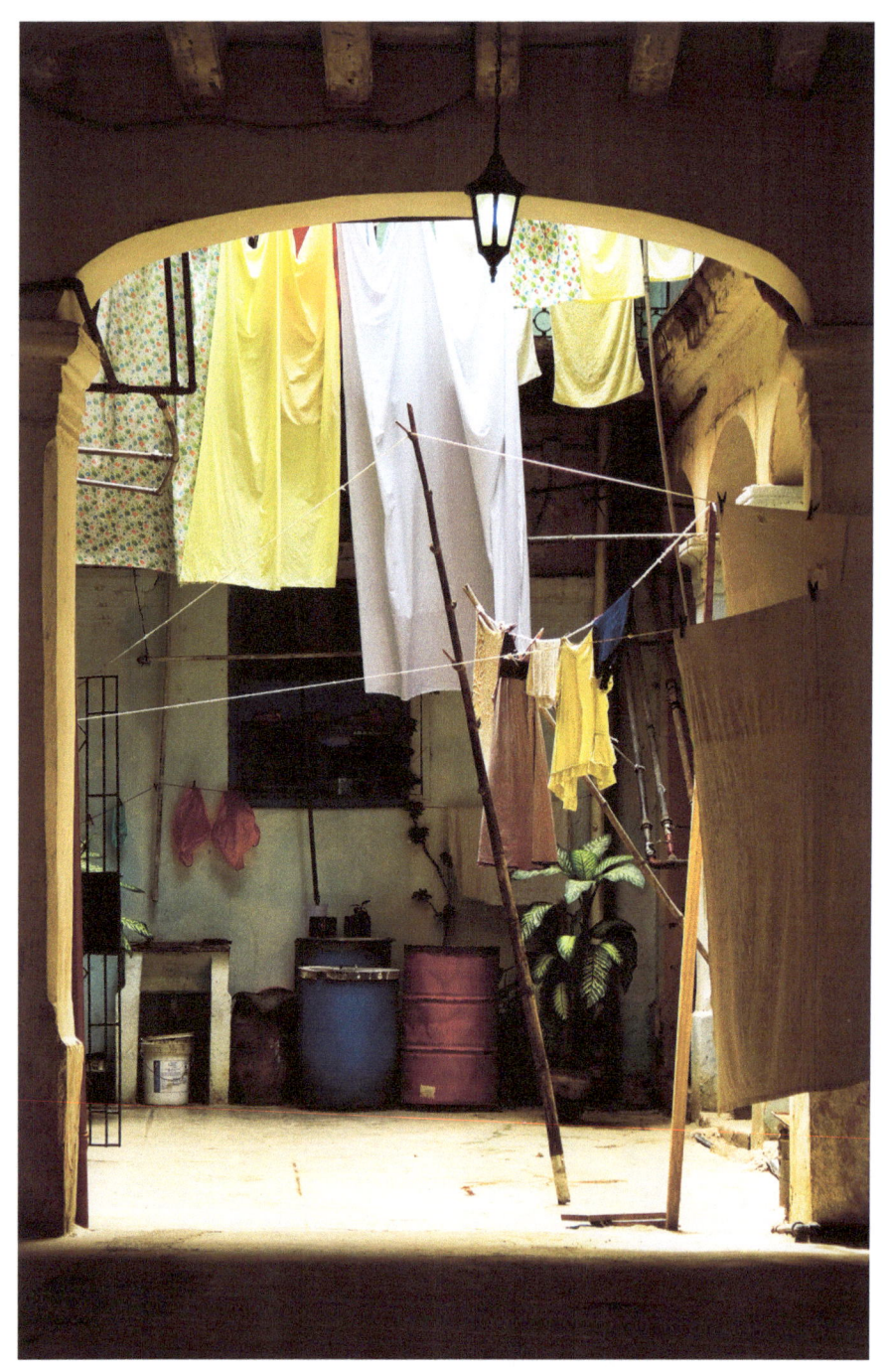

These sunny courtyards are beautiful as well as functional.

Notice a branch and sticks holding up a string so they can hang more clothes to dry. The lack of materials is painfully obvious.

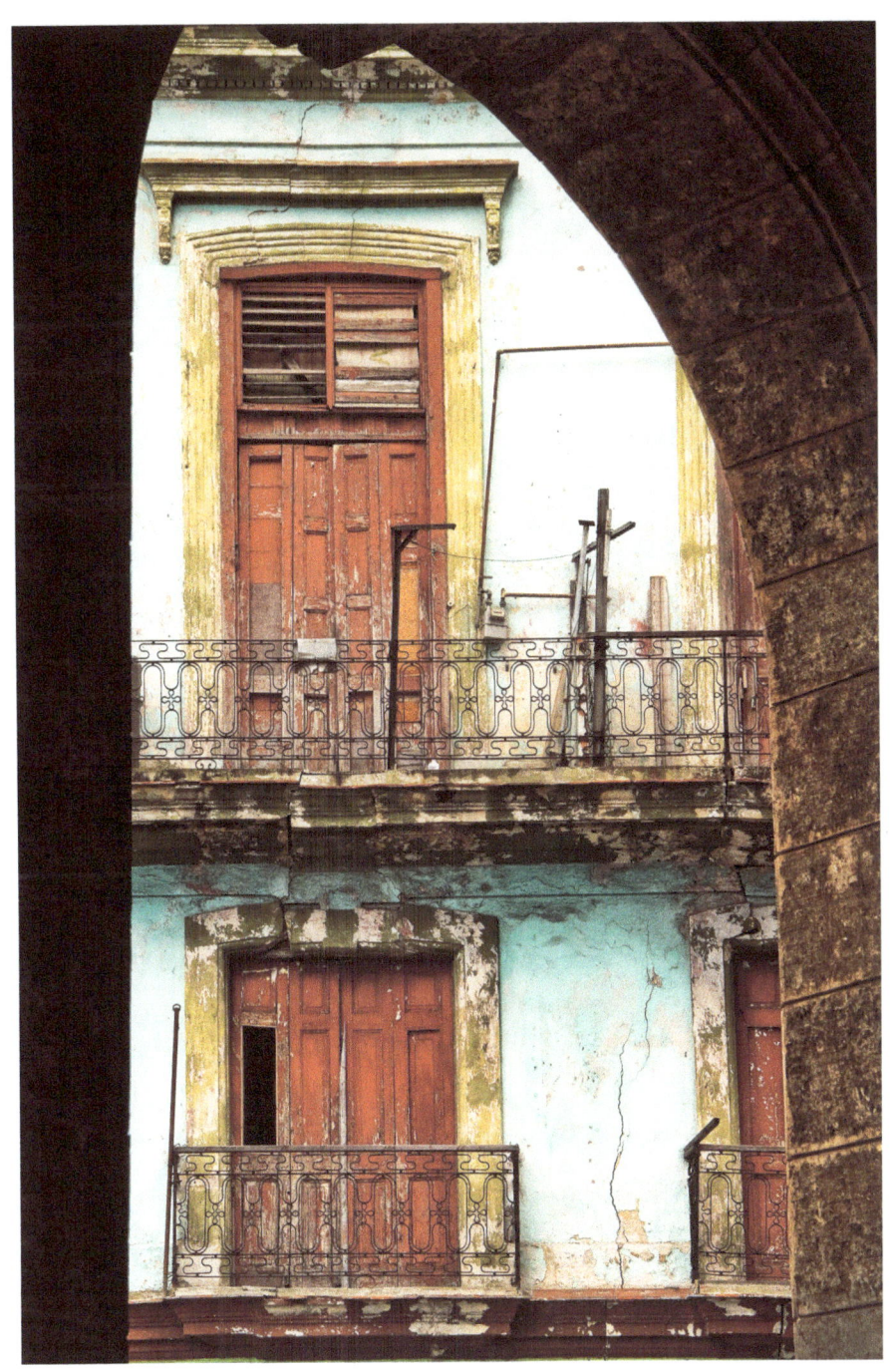

Although many of these buildings are deteriorating, some features, like this balcony's delicate iron work, remain intact and hint at how beautiful they once probably were.

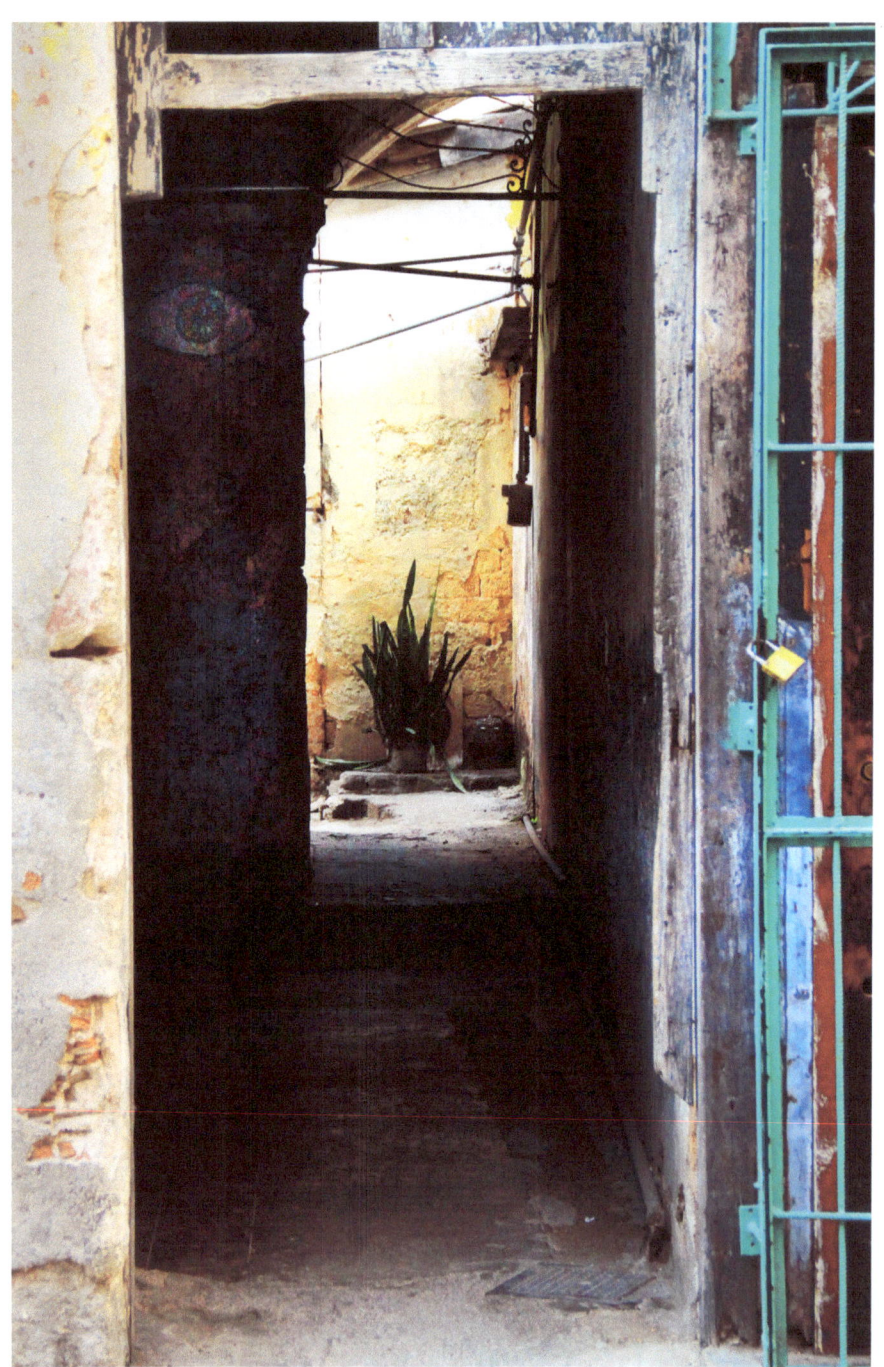

Here is a variation of the courtyard. Instead of the heavy double doors, this one has an iron gate that's painted.

The bright courtyard looks inviting, but the eye on the wall ahead is somewhat dubious, isn't it?

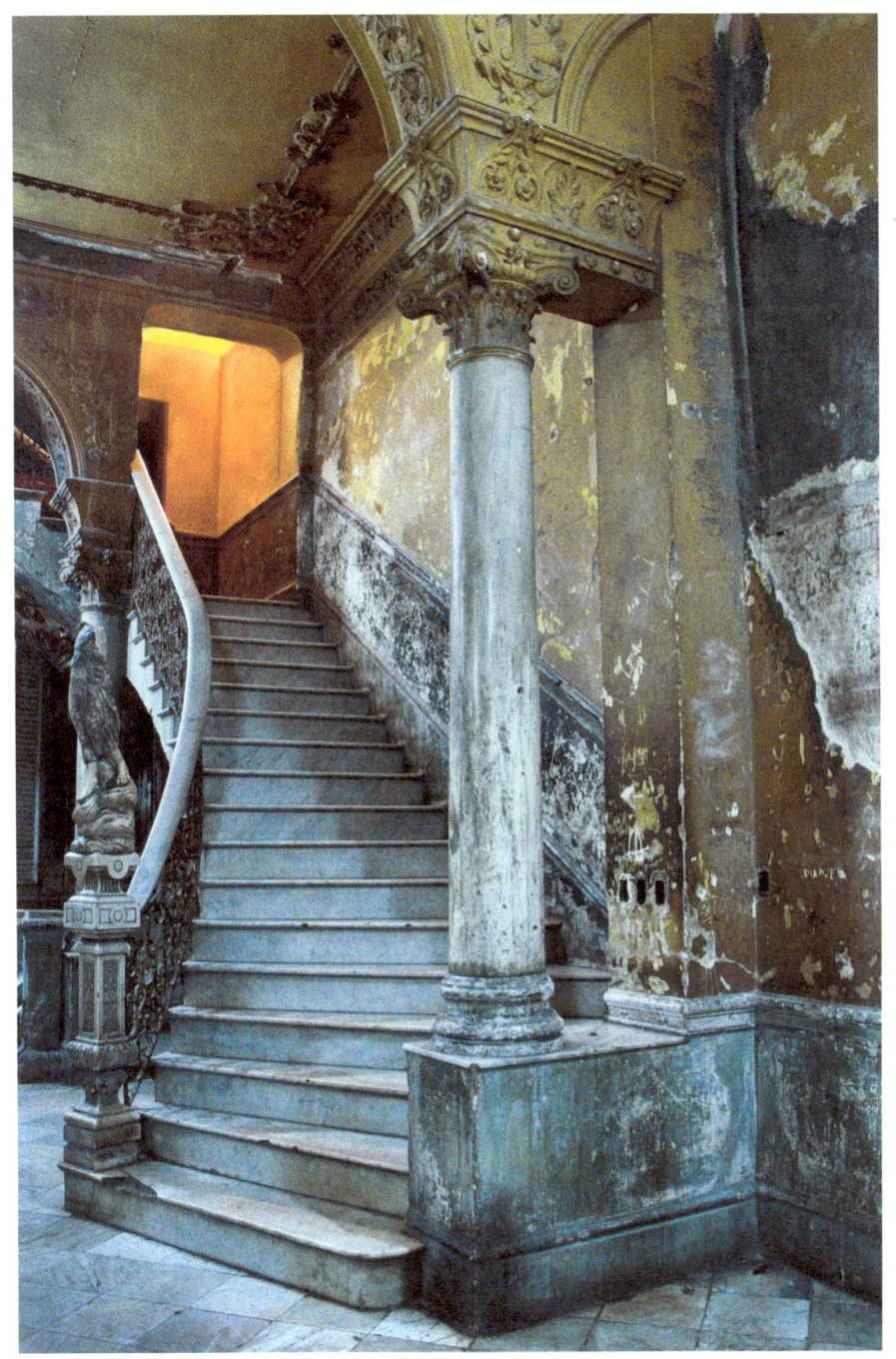

Going inside these neglected buildings provides another glimpse into how impressive these buildings once were.

Here, the paint on the walls is peeling, the marble on the stairs is chipping, and the head of the statue is missing, but it isn't hard to imagine how gorgeous this interior used to be.

However, we must rememer that this was never an average person's home. Fifty-three years of economical hardship and isolation may have caused this decay, but buildings like these were intended for the rich and powerful.

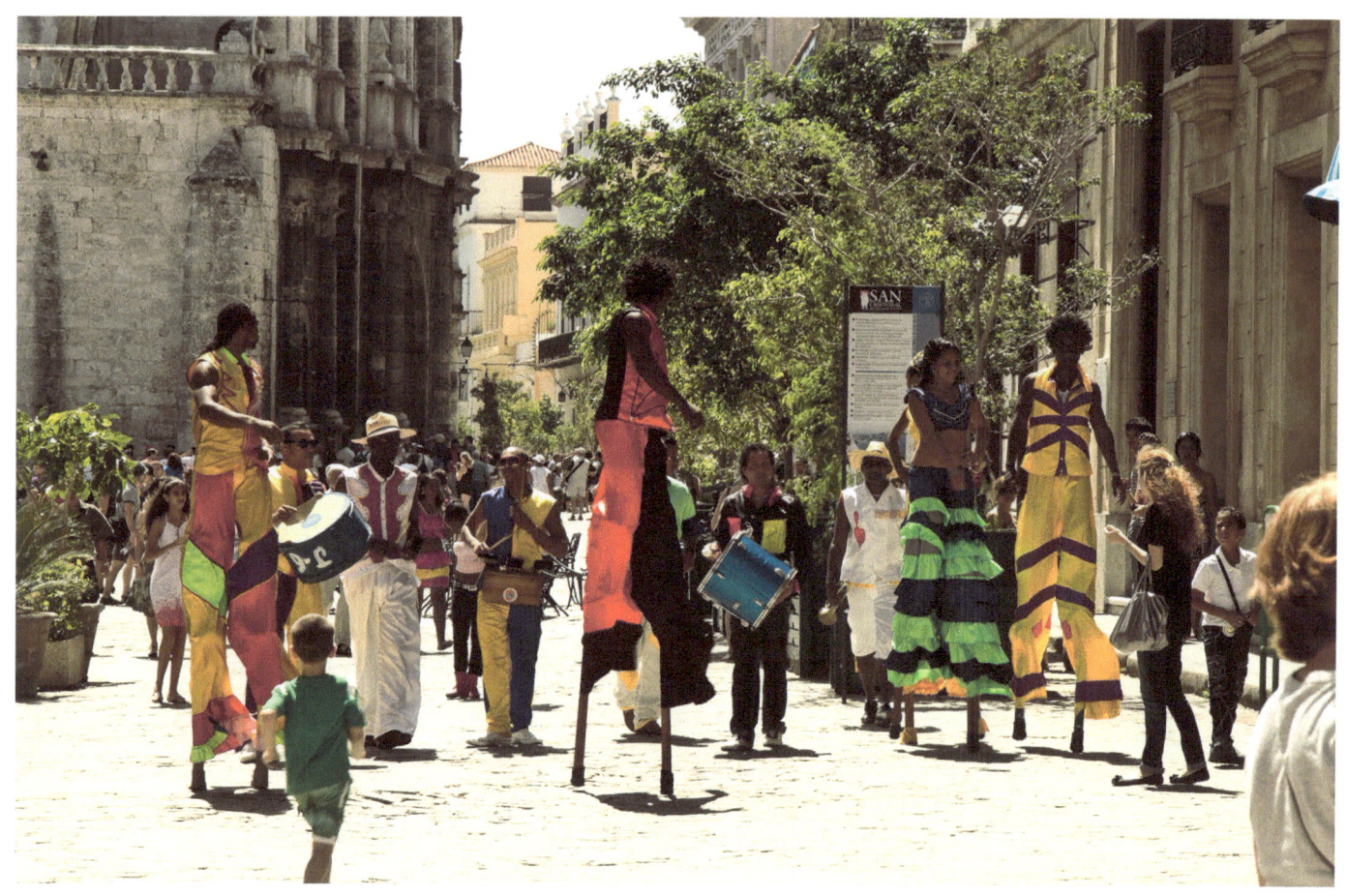

While the average Cuban's life may both minimal and challenging, they still seem to know how to enjoy what they have.

These performers are obviously there for the tourists, but provide entertainment for the neighborhood children as well.

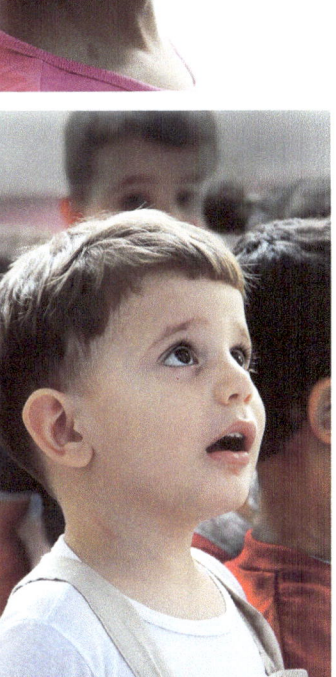
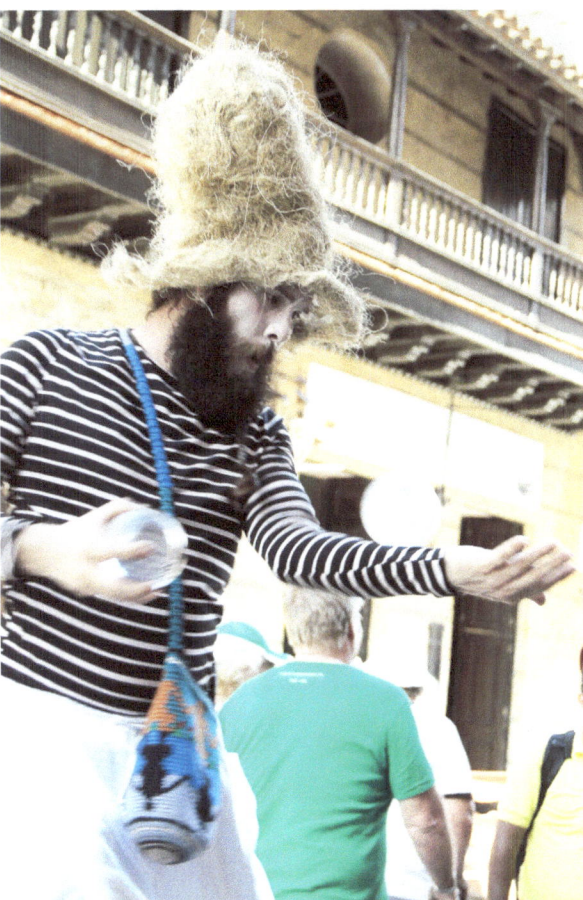
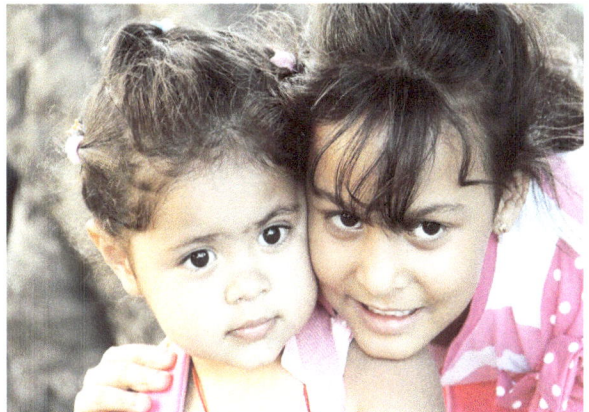
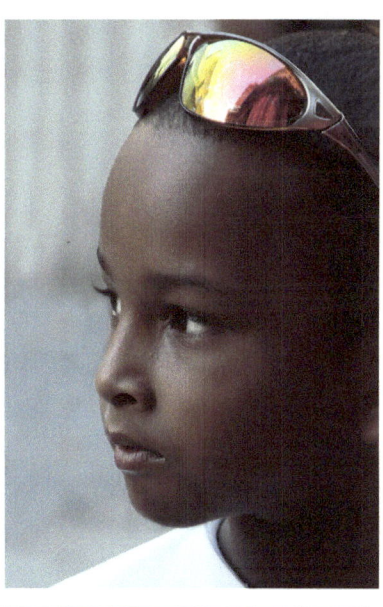
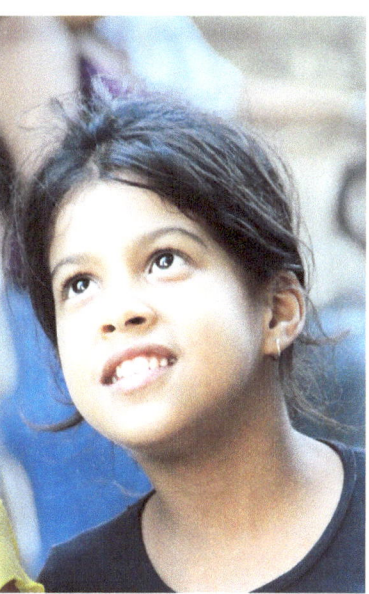

Future of Cuba!

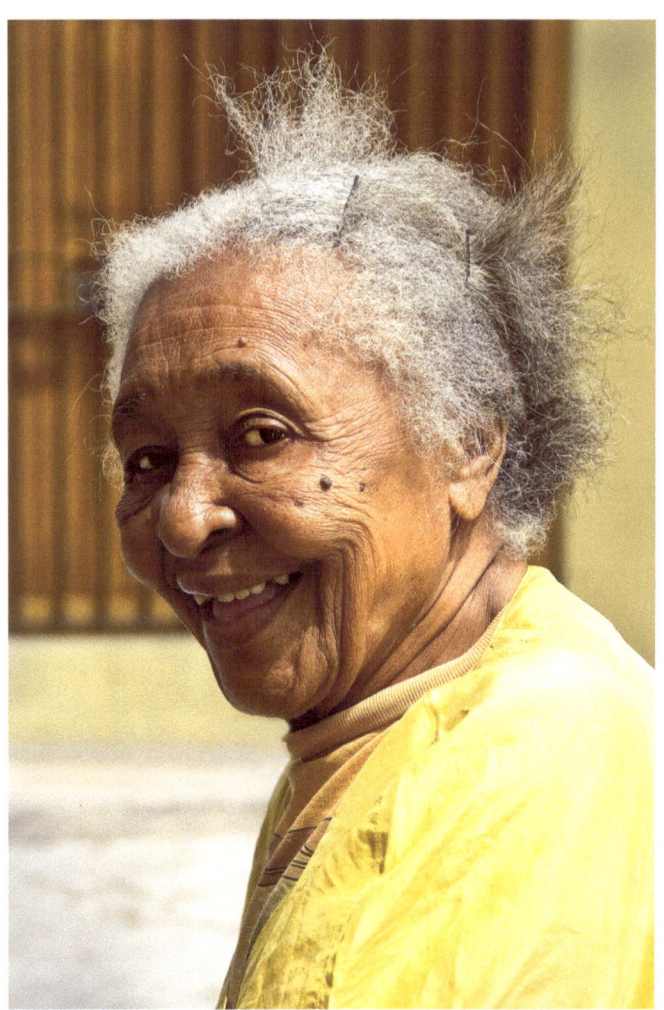 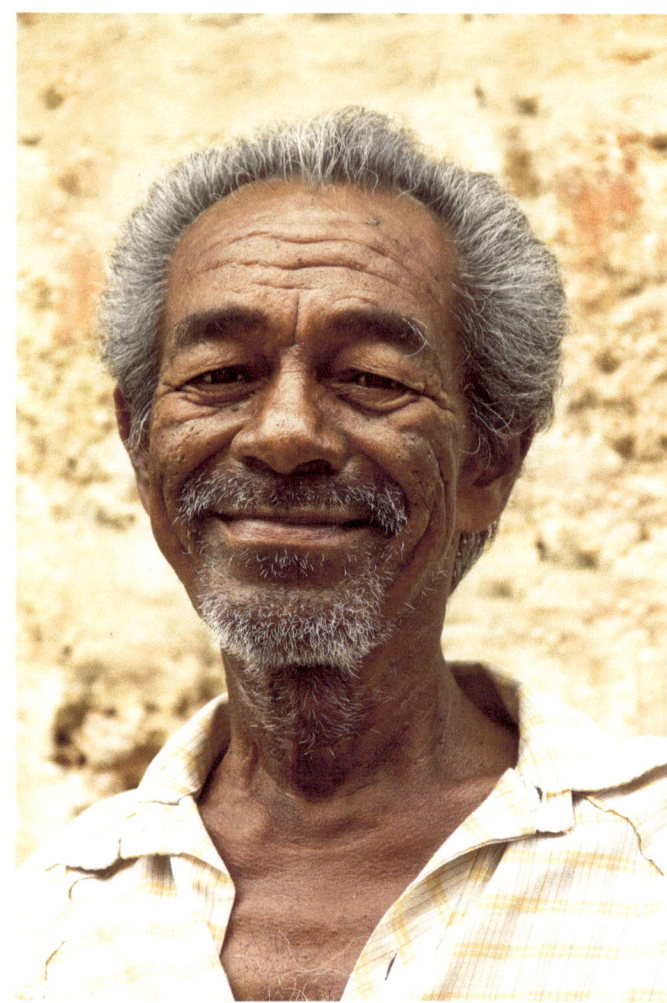

These are the faces of those who have lived through so much and probably struggled all their lives. Although those Cubans who had a lot before the revolution may have lost a lot, they were able to leave Cuba and start new lives. Those who had little before still have little now.

And still, they're smiling. Maybe, if you look closely, you do see sadness in their eyes, but maybe you also see peace.

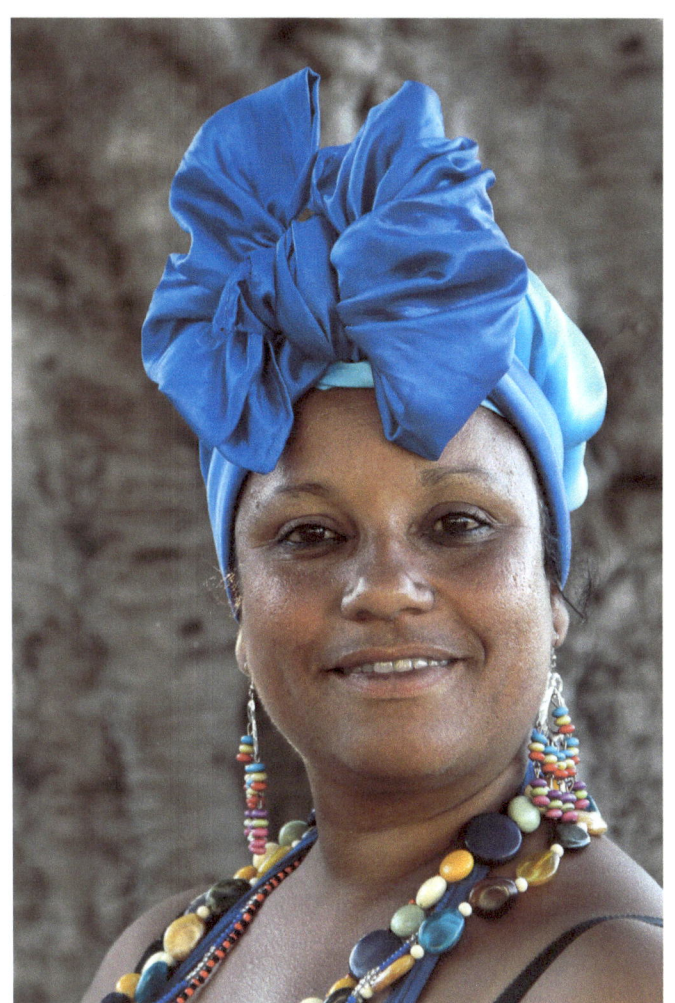 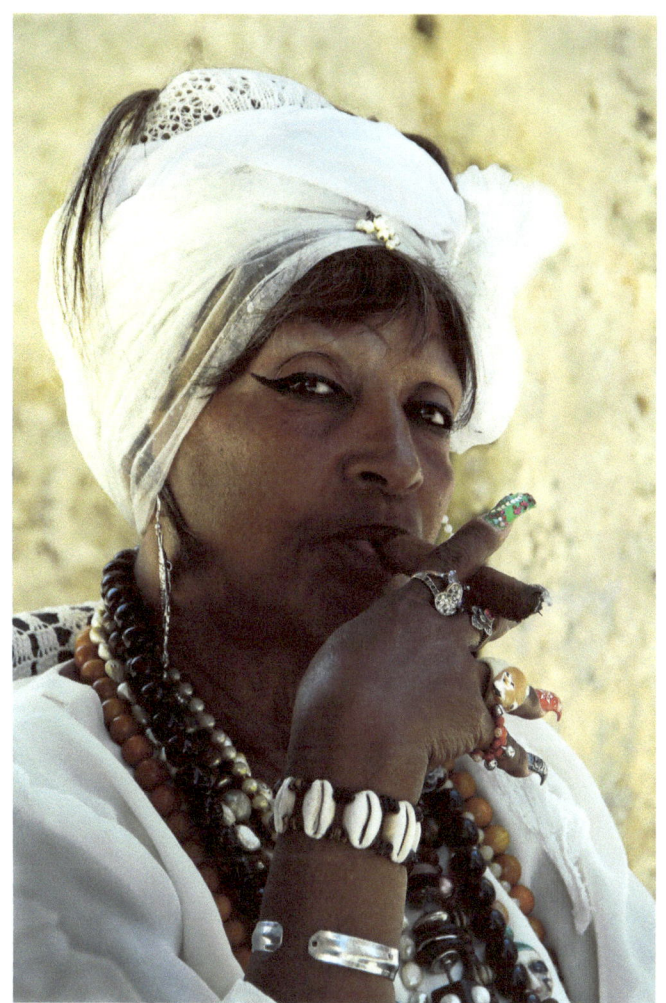

Down in the touristy areas, women adorned in fancy headdresses and jewelry will allow you to take their photo for a convertible peso. Some pose with cigars, but all pose in their own unique style.

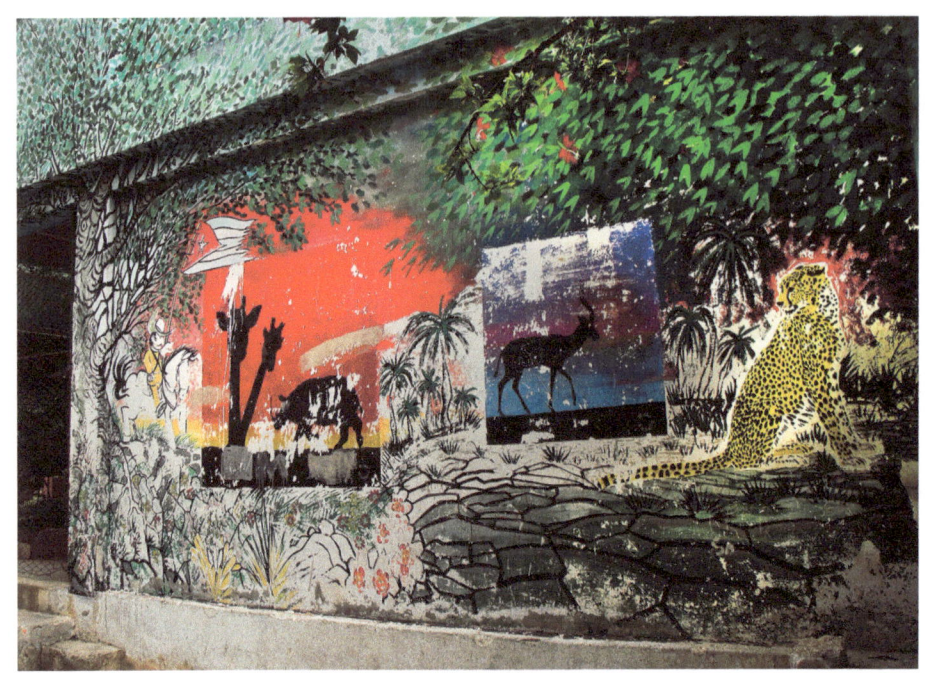

In Havana, colors are everywhere. There are artists whose visions are so big, they cannot be contained in a studio.

Instead, they choose to use the buildings as their canvas, sharing their art with the entire neighbor-hood.

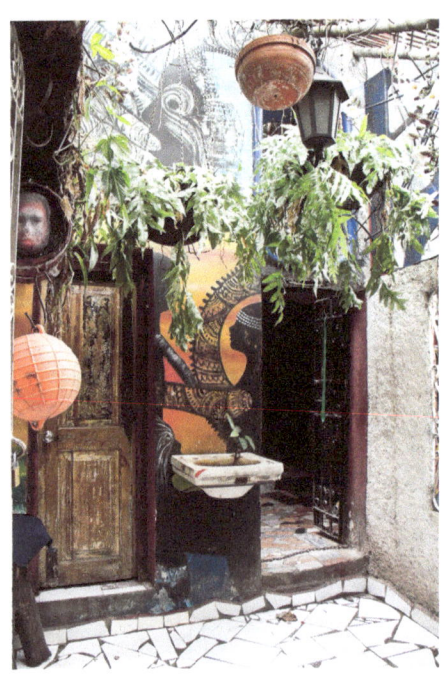

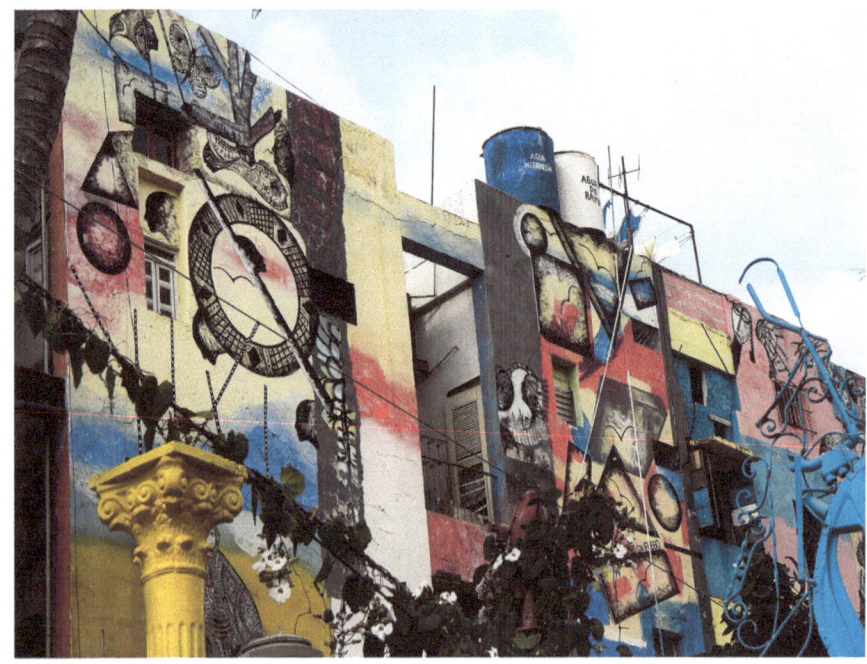

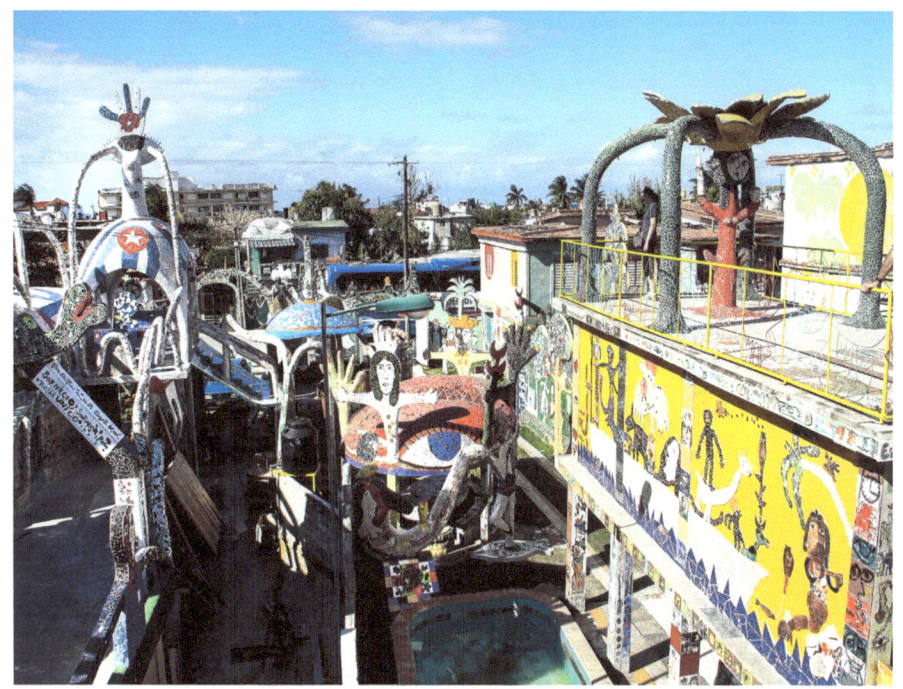

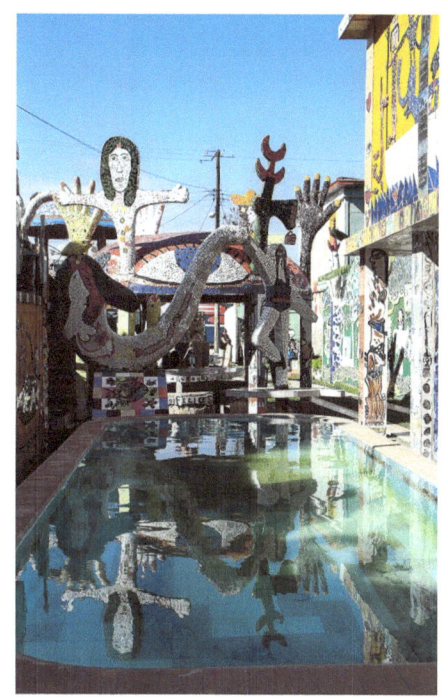

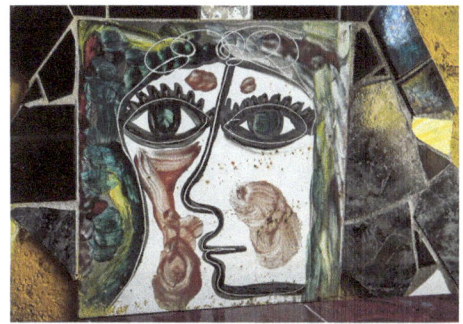

On this block, the artist truly did share his art with the entire neighborhood, covering every open house with thousands of colorful tiles.

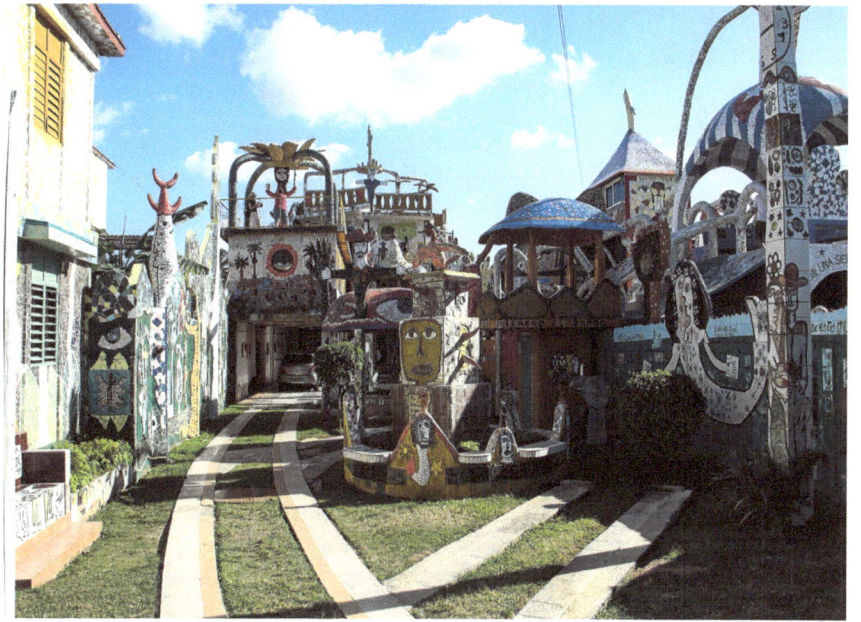

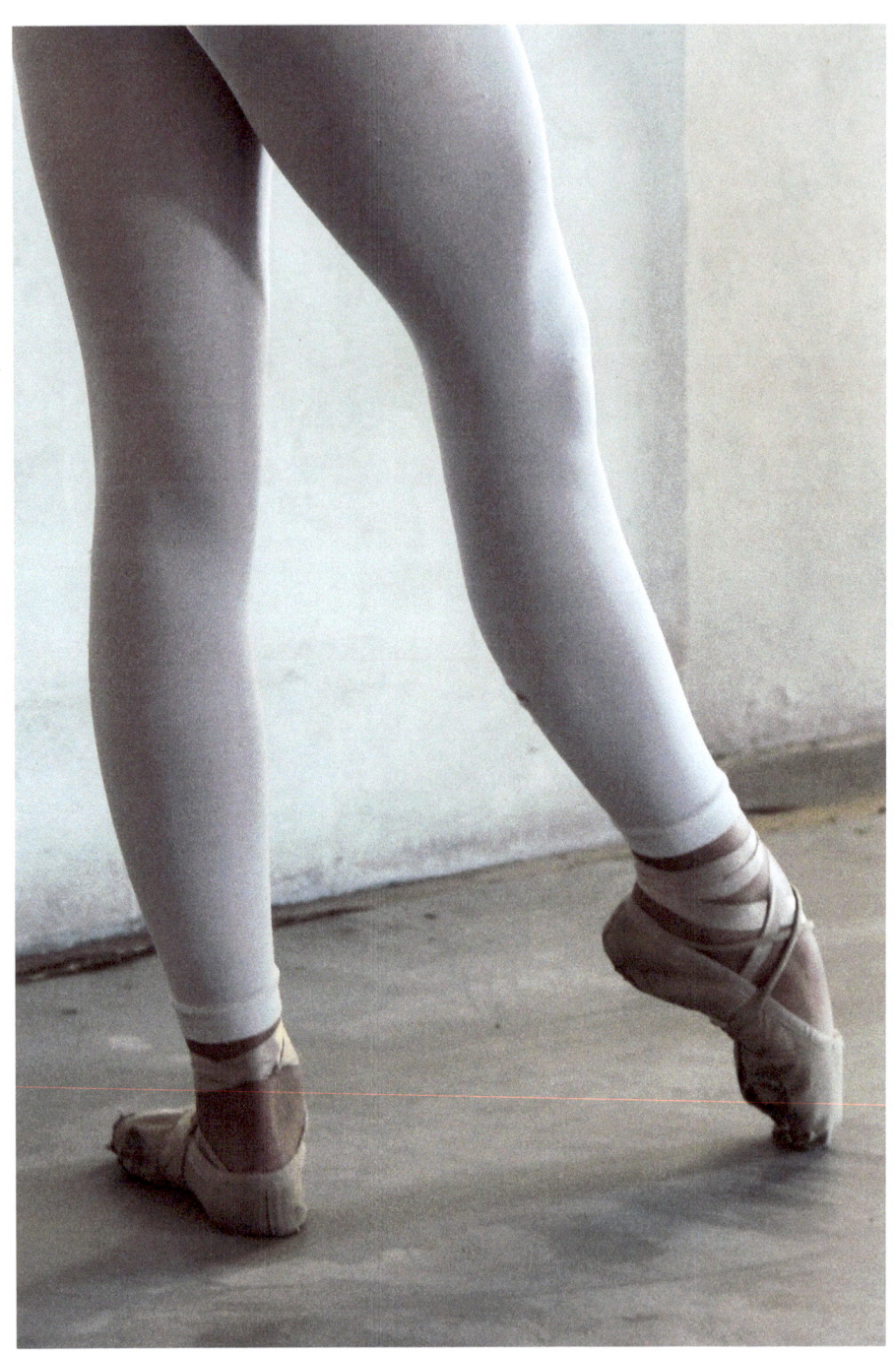

Life may be tough in Havana, but dreams are still big.

In a room full of dancers, the tremendous talent that fills the room distracts from the condition of the building in which they study.

Many of these dancers could follow in the footsteps of Alicia Alonso, a Havana-born ballerina who rose to the international stardom despite an eye defect that left her partially blind.

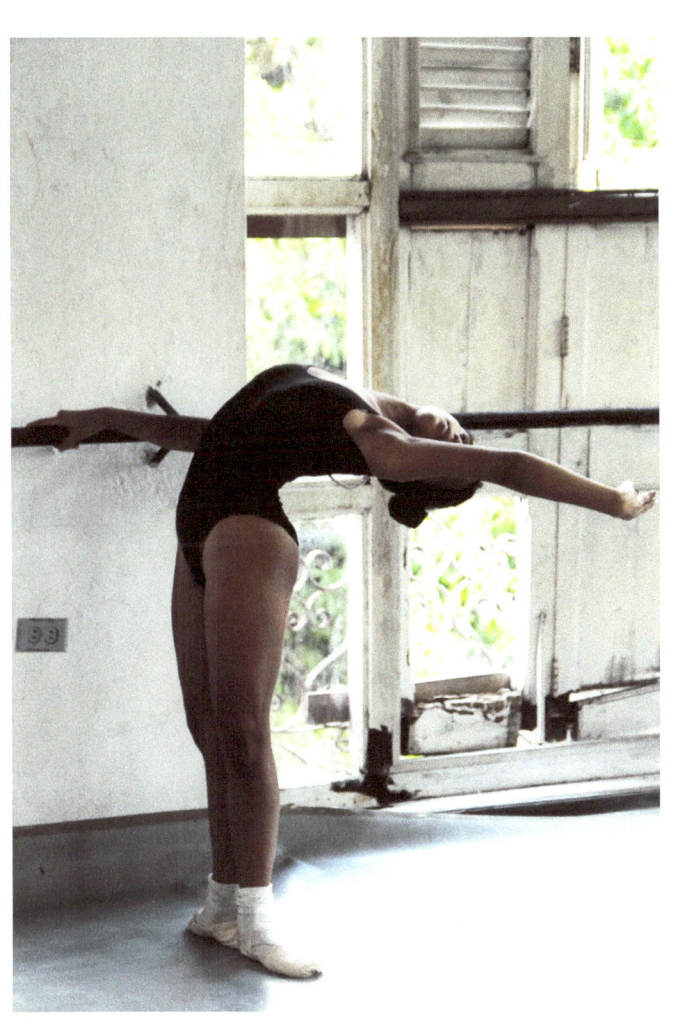
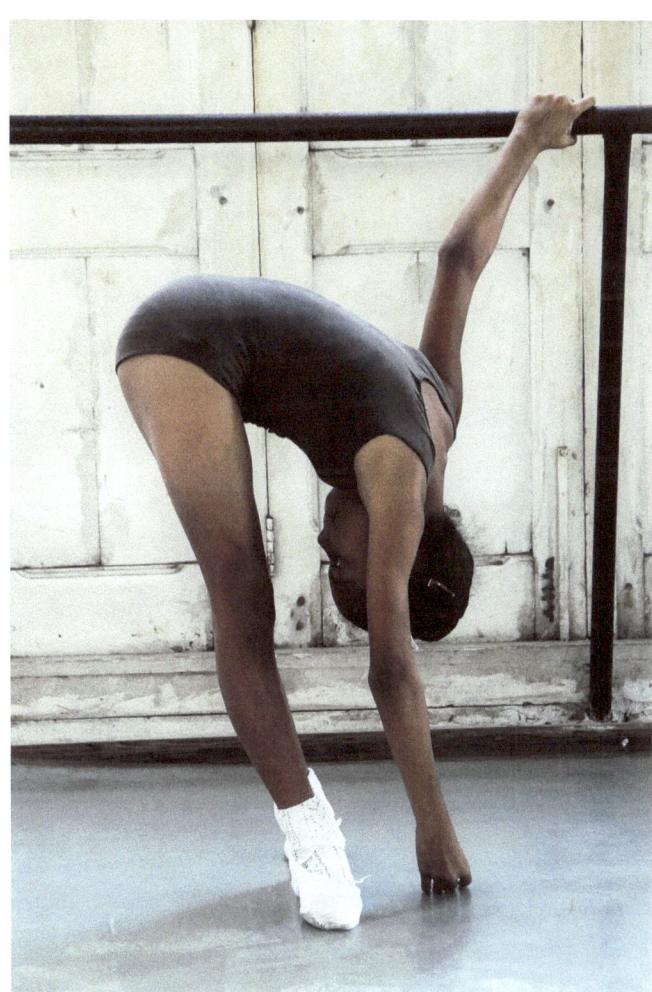

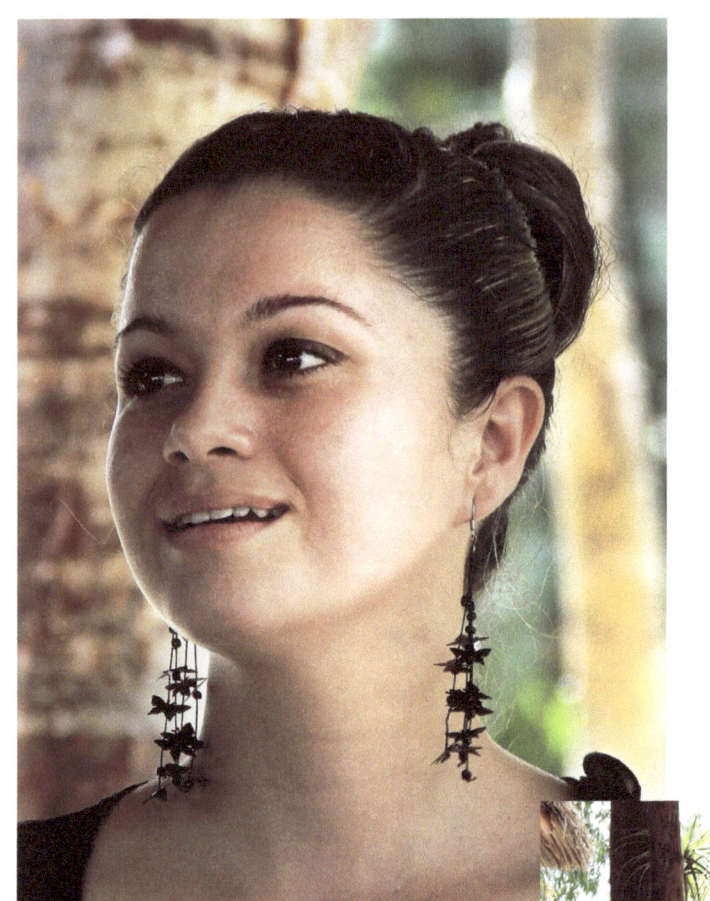

Perhaps it's the music that helps Cubans stay so cheerful.

Of course, you hear some fiery salsa from time to time, but mostly, the music that fills the air is light and pleasant to your ears. Either way, it's hard not to get up and move along to the rhythm.

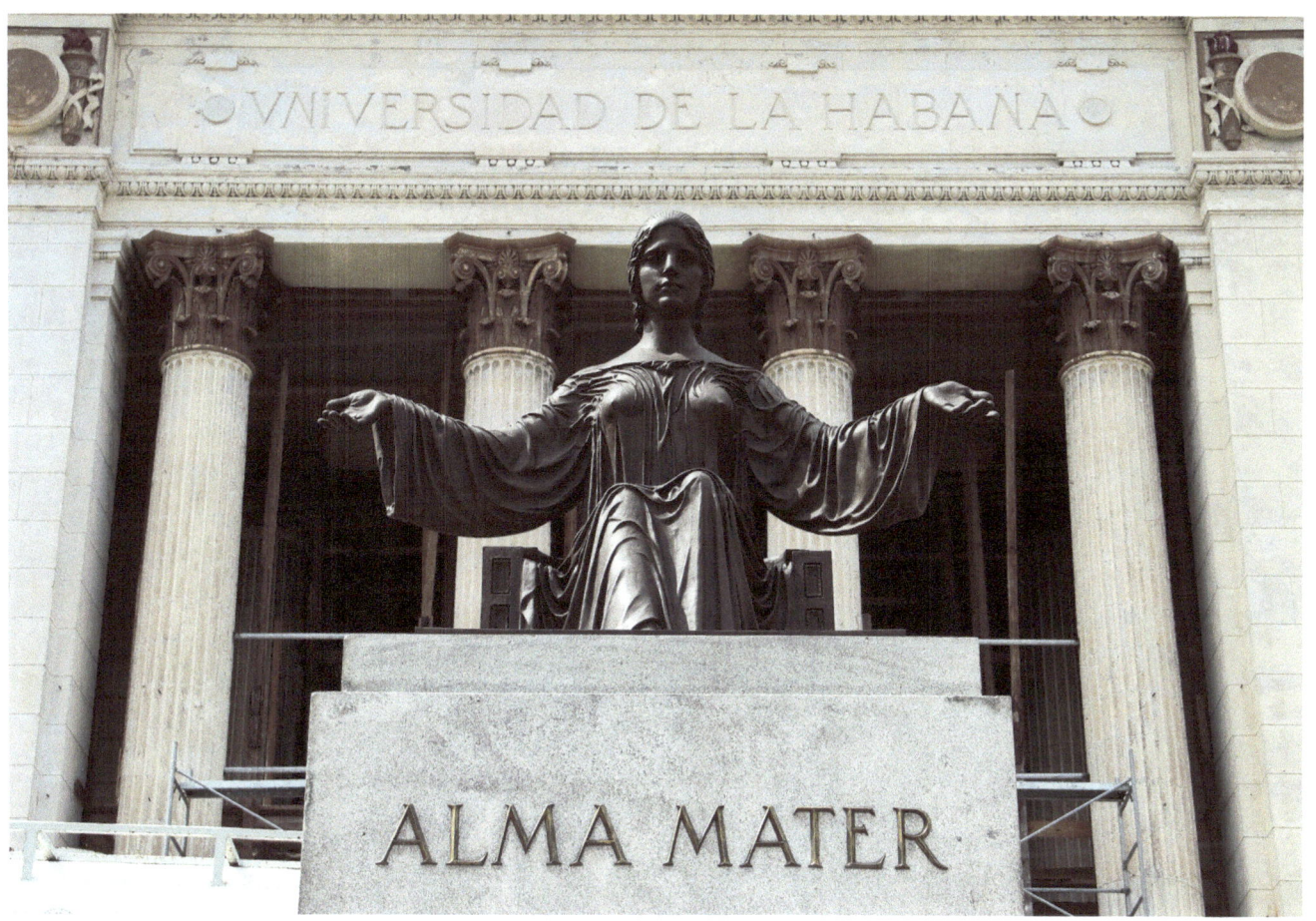

Cuba might be a poor country, but it is not an uneducated one. UNICEF's statistics put Cuba's literacy rate at nearly 100%.

There are bookstores and bookstands everywhere you go, but there is still so much of the world the population cannot access. Once the restrictions are lifted, though, their potential will be endless.

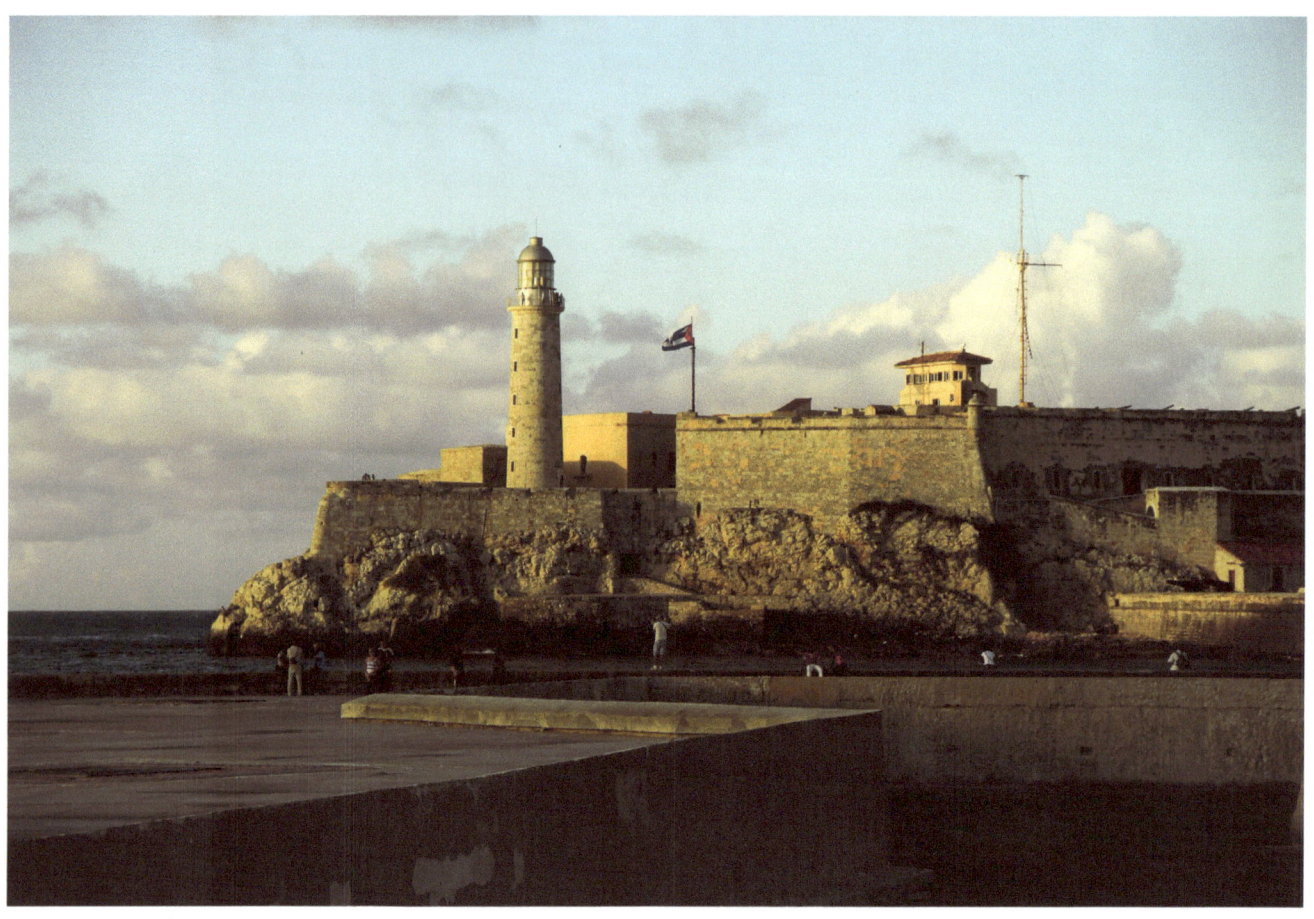

The setting sun lights La Cabana in a warm yellow glow.

Building of this fort began in 1763 by the Spanish to prevent the British colonial power from reaching Havana. Today, powers are coming that will not be stopped by this fort.

No one is talking about it, but everyone can feel it, and the declaration of Good Friday might very well be the first sign that something is happening.

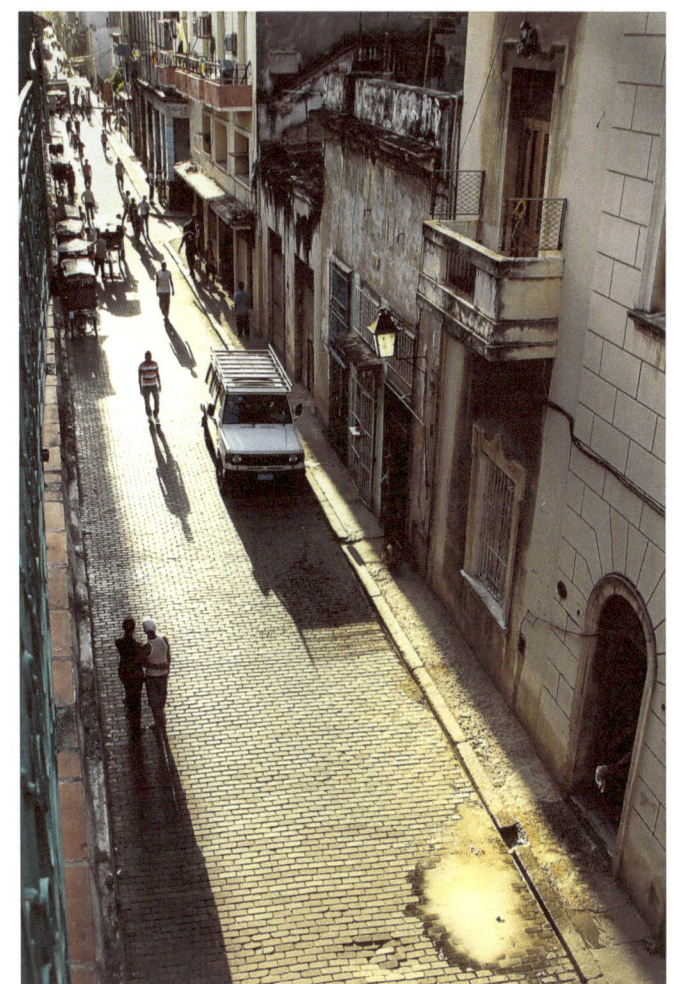 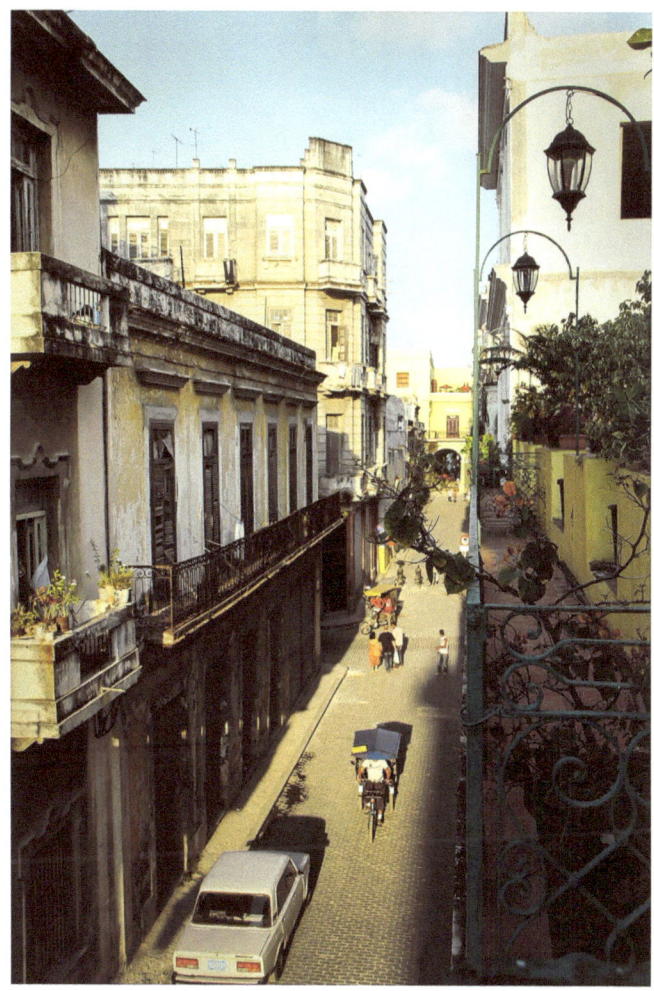

As the shadows get longer, people fill the street again to go home. Of course, this is not the end of a day yet. As the night hides the colors outside, the bright lights will take over in some part of Havana with Jazz and other kinds of music filling the air. But on these streets, where most people live, the double doors will close and the only noise you hear are families talking and laughing.

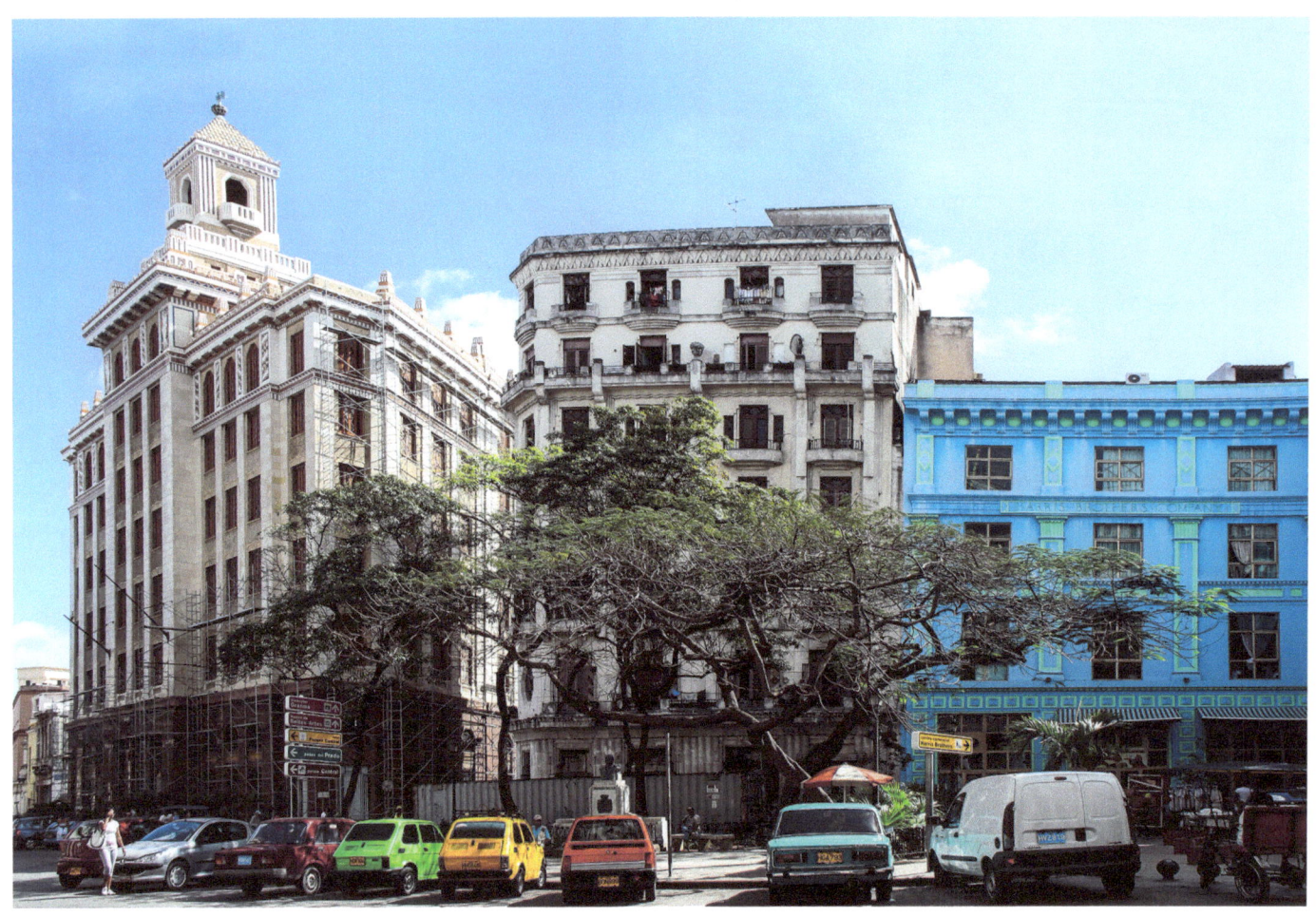

Havana, Cuba is a place where haunting beauty and vibrant energy collide. Soon, there will be changes and these crumbling buildings may become a thing of the past. Let's just hope that those beautiful smiles never disappear.

Like many others who have visited Cuba, I would love to return many more times.

www.ingramcontent.com/pod-product-compliance
Lightning Source LLC
Chambersburg PA
CBHW050402180526
45159CB00005B/2120